HOW TO BECOME A
GARDENER

Brimming with creative inspiration, how-to projects, and useful information to enrich your everyday life, quarto.com is a favorite destination for those pursuing their interests and passions.

First Published in 2023 by Cool Springs Press, an imprint of The Quarto Group,
100 Cummings Center, Suite 265-D, Beverly, MA 01915, USA.
T (978) 282-9590 F (978) 283-2742 Quarto.com

Cool Springs Press titles are also available at discount for retail, wholesale, promotional, and bulk purchase. For details, contact the Special Sales Manager by email at specialsales@quarto.com or by mail at The Quarto Group, Attn: Special Sales Manager, 100 Cummings Center, Suite 265-D, Beverly, MA 01915, USA.

27 26 25 24 23   1 2 3 4 5

ISBN: 978-0-7603-7424-5

Digital edition published in 2023
eISBN: 978-0-7603-7425-2

Library of Congress Cataloging-in-Publication Data is available.

Design and Page Layout: Laura Klynstra
Photography: Takia Lamb except those noted in the photo credits on page 198

Printed in China

HOW TO BECOME A
GARDENER

Find
EMPOWERMENT
in creating
your own
FOOD SECURITY

ASHLIE THOMAS, The Mocha Gardener

COOL
SPRINGS
PRESS

PRAISE

"Bursting with encouragement, information, and heart and woven together through colorful photography, *How to Become a Gardener* is an inspiring roadmap that will guide you to become a conscious and grateful steward of your burgeoning garden, both inside and out."

—Meg Cowden, @seedtofork, author of *Plant Grow Harvest Repeat*

"*How to Become a Gardener* covers the basics of how to start a garden from scratch for the first-time gardener, provides advice and emotional support to help through the challenges, and dives into the philosophy behind why gardening can transform our lives in the most beautiful of ways. With this book we can not only transform our lives and take control of our health but also overcome food insecurity and create resilient communities. Unlike many gardening books, Ashlie is inclusive of our most vulnerable communities, making this book a true solution for many who are often left out of the conversation. To grow our own food is to begin the transformation of ourselves and our communities. *How to Become a Gardener* is the tool of empowerment that is needed by so many to begin this transformation."

—Rob Greenfield, environmental activist and author of *Food Freedom*

"Absolute must-read! This book perfectly highlights the value of food security and health. It gives the tools to empower anyone to change their lives through food. I will be recommending this book to all my patients!"

—Cierra Allen-Dixon, MD

"Ashlie's book is a timely, in-depth look at gardening as a way to fight food insecurity and provides encouragement to grow in any environment with limited space to meet cultural food needs. She offers a thoughtfully written, well-researched beginner's guide to gardening as a means to equalize access to healthy, nutritious foods. Her book is truly a blueprint for increasing access to healthy foods and combating the food swamps so prevalent today."

—Claudia Weekes, MS RD LD, @theorganizedhomemaker

"Ashlie's approach to 'creating your own food security' is so critical and empowering in this time when so many lack access to adequate healthy food and have lost touch with the wonders of the natural world. This book is an outstanding but practical guide to how each of us can contribute to our own destiny and to the betterment of society by planting seeds in our backyard or even in a pot on our back porch."

—Dr. Alice S. Ammerman, professor of nutrition and director of the Center for Health Promotion and Disease Prevention, University of North Carolina at Chapel Hill, founder of Equiti Foods

"*How to Become a Gardener* has everything you need to not just grow your own food but to become a steward of community and food justice. Ashlie's passion and perspective are so beautifully encapsulated in this book, and her lived experience shows just how intertwined our food system is to our own empowerment. It combines science with practical tips and stories from her own green journey as she explores what it means to nurture the gardens within us."

—Nick Cutsumpas, author, television personality, and founder of Farmer Nick

DEDICATION

To my husband, Tyler, who has supported me throughout this journey and helped me materialize all of the crazy ideas I had and continue to have for our garden. I admire you and I am proud to have you as my life partner and my confidant. To my family, who reminds me each day of who I am and where I come from, I thank you for loving me without bounds. To my friends, mentors, and colleagues, I appreciate you all contributing in your own way to the construction of this work. Whether it was through conversations over tea, brainstorming sessions, or simple words of encouragement and inspiration, I am grateful for all of it.

Finally, to anyone with a curiosity of learning how to begin gardening or how to gain greater freedom over your food options through gardening, I leave you with this encouraging quote from edible gardening advocate and author Lauri Kranz, "When you feel like everything is out of control, what nurtures better than planting a seed with the promise of bounty and health that comes with it?"

Growing food gives us the ability to choose and consume what is best for our bodies and with greater Intentionality and awareness.

CONTENTS

INTRODUCTION

The Journey to Becoming a Gardener

Gardening is a vital part of my well-being and journey to living a full and healthy life. Several years ago, my husband Tyler and I began our gardening journey on our one-acre North Carolina homestead. Together, we dreamed, designed, and built this garden from a blank slate, meaning nothing but unleveled grass and dense forest. Our modest 1950s suburban home in Graham is nestled between three major cities: Chapel Hill, Durham, and Greensboro. Though we enjoy the charm and calm nature of this small city, we are a bit of distance away from cities with greater food diversity. Interestingly, this is not the first time I have experienced a lack of nutritional diversity. After spending many years in a deeply rural South Carolina town that lacked sufficient access to nutritious foods, I realized one way to address this barrier may be through learning how to grow my own food and educating others on what quality foods consist of and from where they originate.

This experience of living in rural South Carolina was what many may call a turning point for me. I began to understand that the growing issue of food security is a continuum with nonlinear variables for its cause. The face of this complex issue is not always clear, but the implications are almost always reflective in the health outcomes of communities, especially the most vulnerable ones. The challenges associated with food security are undeniably complicated and multilayered, but growing up I was told that sometimes the best way to eat away at big problems is through taking small, gradual bites.

Opposite: The journey to becoming a gardener embodies a holistic evolution of the mind, body, and spirit. I welcome this transformation with open arms and gratitude.

With a bit of imagination and planning, you can design and create your own food-filled haven using the space you have.

Over time, I developed a profound desire to disrupt the local food systems in communities that lacked access to wholesome and nutritious sustenance that the body needs to thrive. You see, I wanted more for my family and more for my community, so I figured one small step toward this ambition of empowering and creating greater food autonomy and resilience would be through guiding individuals to explore, grow, and connect with delicious foods produced by their own hands. I believe that gardening presents the opportunity to do just that.

A friend who is a veteran gardener told me, "Gardening is a never-ending experience of enlightenment," and through this journey I am willing to bet that you may recognize an enlightenment will take place within yourself as well. I can honestly say that as I embarked upon the quest of learning to grow my own food, I became more conscious of local food systems, and the health of myself, those around me, and the environment. Additionally, while constructing our garden, Tyler and I sought to build a haven that served as a spiritually enlightening place to ground and regenerate, not just for ourselves, but for anyone who entered the space. I truly believe that gardens can be places that promote strength and healing, and we wanted our space to do just that. I am also thankful that our garden gives us an opportunity to connect with and give honor to what we feed ourselves and those around us (human and nonhuman). Even the mere act of caring for a garden has allowed me to foster a lovely holistic and symbiotic relationship with nature—I nurture the green life around me, and it nurtures me in return.

In this book, I offer insights on how caring for a garden, especially an edible one, may lead to a greater relationship with nature and food that is based upon resilience, reciprocity, and respect. Your path to becoming a gardener will be unique and filled with individualized lessons, but know that you are not alone. There are so many gardeners all around the world learning just like you and me. Throughout my gardening quest, I have discovered that becoming a gardener is a wonderful metamorphic process that requires much of ourselves, but it gives much more in return. As you move through this book, I welcome you to imagine us walking through a garden together, mine or perhaps a vision of your own garden. And at the end of our journey together, it is my hope that you depart feeling edified and encouraged to take control of your well-being through growing the very thing that sustains you: good, nutritious food.

Opposite: You may find that your garden becomes a sanctuary that is warm, welcoming, and filled with endless possibilities.

We constructed this space with the intention of growing good food for ourselves and those around us. We grew this garden, and in return the garden grew us.

In 2019, the area that is now the garden was nothing but gently sloping land with dense forestry in the back. Together we built our garden from the ground up.

CHAPTER 1

A GARDEN DEFINED

What Makes a Space a Garden?

What is the first thing that comes to mind when you hear the word "garden"? Many may say that a garden is a place where flowers and/or vegetables grow, and they would certainly be correct. Technically speaking, a garden is a designated and planned space used for cultivating and nurturing plants and other forms of nature. However, I believe that the term embodies that definition and so much more. If I had to articulate my perception of what a garden is, it would be along the lines of this: a garden is an intentional space that seeks to cultivate organismal collaboration, respect, and sustainability within an ecosystem. This perspective emphasizes the importance of protecting not only the health and well-being of humans, but also other valuable organisms within ecosystems. In order for a garden to thrive, we have to work together and seek to understand the value that every organism brings to the ecological table.

Now, let's dive into what this organismal collaboration and respect may consist of, shall we? If I had to think about the various species that I come across while I'm in the garden, I could easily list them: plants, common earthworms, birds, bees, frogs, and mushrooms are a few that come to mind (by the way, I have a story about the frogs that will come later on in the book). But the one thing that gardening teaches me is to look closely at the role each of these species plays, not just in the garden, but in the totality of the ecosystem. What may seem so small and perhaps insignificant may present a vital component to the balance within nature.

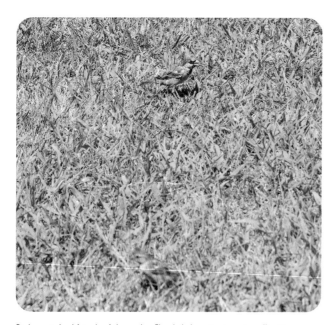

Birds are indeed friends of the garden. They help by eating insects, pollinating flowering plants, and energizing the space with birdsongs.

It may be common knowledge that the essence of a garden is plants, and trust me, there are several hundreds of thousands of species of plants. However, there are many more types of organisms, which tend to occasionally slip our memory, that may help in the development of gardens. For instance, the earthworms. These slimy, slithering annelids increase soil porosity and promote nutrient cycling through compost production. Then there are the insect pollinators, such as the butterflies and bees, that not only support plant diversity but also play a major role in helping to fertilize plants that ultimately mature into the foods we eat. Next are the frogs, which I like to refer to as the amphibious indicator species of ecosystem health. If something has gone awry in the area, look out for the behavior of the frogs. Additionally, this particular animal serves as prey and predator, meaning they are vital for insect control, while also serving as a food source for other larger wildlife. Now, if we dig a bit deeper, we will find microbes or living microscopic organisms within the soil that we cannot see with our naked eye most of the time. Microbes, like bacteria and fungi, promote sustainable biospheres as

decomposers, where they're able to break down and recycle dead organic matter into nutrients that the soil needs. So, you see, a healthy and collaborative ecosystem sets the foundation for a flourishing garden.

Another way to show respect for the various organisms within the ecosystem is by being cognizant of the native species that are around us. Though there are a wide variety of plants that may be used in a garden plot, the best types are either edible or decorative plants that are native to or compatible with the local climate. When introduced to a new environment, nonnative organisms, despite being incredibly intriguing at times, can directly and indirectly affect biotic factors and disrupt essential ecological functions. Meaning, when plants or other organisms (such as insects, bacteria, or even seeds) are introduced into a new ecosystem, their mere existence can alter biodiversity, shift soil chemistry, or even pose a threat to food and resources for native wildlife and humans. This is particularly true if nonnative species possess invasive characteristics or the ability to dominate space and resources. The good news is that there is great value in researching our local habitats. Topics such as weather patterns, soil composition, plant guides, and much more are readily available and accessible online, in books, in databases, and through local university- or government-based agricultural services.

We can see that there are many types of species that must work together to foster a healthy and balanced ecosystem, and gardening has the ability to serve as a practice of good environmental stewardship. Simply put, our actions, no matter how small or large, can significantly impact the natural habitat around us. If we are good to the earth, the earth will be good to us in return.

Now, I'm sure that I'm not alone when I say that as the garden grows, so does the gardener. Like the plants in the garden, there are many aspects of our physical, mental, and spiritual selves that may begin to sprout and mature or transform. I can certainly attest to this transformation, whether it was inten-

We should seek to build a haven not just for ourselves, but for the life around us as well.

tional or not, and I am deeply appreciative for it. Tyler and I built this garden with the intention of it serving as a meditative space that mentally and physically feeds us and those around us. To be fair, there have been many times when we have wanted to throw in the towel due to the learning curve, time conflicts, and simply frustration, but that is where the journey lies—in overcoming all these things and pressing forward toward the goal of food sovereignty. To this day, we have not been disappointed with the fruits of our labor—nor will you be. As you embark upon your own journey toward becoming a gardener and obtaining greater food autonomy (this concept is highlighted in greater detail in chapter 2), you may find that there is much work involved in designing and preparing a green growing space of your own, but with proper planning, research, and a bit of imagination, you will be empowered to create it.

HOW SHOULD YOU BEGIN?

The first step in constructing your garden is planning in advance and properly researching your property or space. I emphasize proper research because there is a great deal of information available on gardening, but one way to narrow the scope of everything is to focus on information that is relevant to what you have and what you hope to accomplish. For this reason, a good initial focus is understanding the environment that you live in. Topographical features, existing plants and wildlife, the local climate, soil composition, and nearby structures are all details that will determine not only the type of garden that's best for your desired space, but also what will grow optimally. For months Tyler and I walked around the backyard of our home, mentally designing the layout of our future garden. During this time, we really pulled on our strengths. I, with a technical science background, thoroughly enjoyed organizing and researching books and articles related to gardening and growing food. Tyler, who has a background in construction, enjoyed composing and building things from the ground up. It took us several months to get started because we had recently moved into our home, and we wanted to get a feel for the property and habitat, which we knew would take time. Evaluating the current state of our property allowed us to figure out ways to enhance what was already there, as we desired to complement the ecosystem around us, not subtract from it.

During our planning, we wanted to address several logistical aspects before getting started. Understanding the climate was the first priority. Here in the Piedmont region of North Carolina, the climate conditions are known to have a minimum average temperature of 5°F to 10°F (-15°C to -12°C), with frost dates ranging between November and mid-April. This climate fact is important to know because it means that this area has a fairly long growing season for a variety of trees, flowers, and vegetables. Furthermore, knowing the characteristics of our climate helped us understand which plants would

After months of planning, we opted to build nine wooden raised beds because our native soil would require extensive remediation to prepare for a garden.

grow well. Our second priority was researching topographical features and soil (which is discussed in greater depth in chapter 3). Not all soil is the same everywhere, so we had to consider the type of soil that was best to use in our garden. Naturally, the soil composition in this region consists of a mixture between clay and sand, also known as Cecil clay. This means that it's hard as a rock when dry but mushy when wet. Cecil clay is fertile, moderately permeable, and well-draining; however, the surface layer has a dark gray sandy loam consistency while the subsoil is a deep orange or red clay loam. Additionally, there was a vast number of rocks that rested beneath the surface. Needless to say, we found out quickly that this was not the easiest soil to work with, so we opted to use garden beds and began brainstorming the types of beds we would need for the various vegetables and plants we sought to grow.

What you choose to start your garden with is completely up to you. For instance, my sister and brother-in-law use a mix of raised and container beds to cultivate a food and flower garden in their backyard.

One last planning tip that we made sure to consider was understanding our property orientation, boundaries, and existing structures. Because our property is more than eighty years old, there are many well-established deciduous and nut trees, so we got a chance to monitor how they influenced the access to and orientation of light throughout the year. And though there is a degree of charm associated with having a mid-century home, this also comes with some uncertainties, like not having an accurate record of the property's boundaries and belowground infrastructures. Nevertheless, we were able to contact professional agencies and surveyors to gather this information and assist us in mapping out the location of water pipes and gas lines, and the above structures like power lines. I highlight my planning experience to show how all these factors can influence the type and function of the garden that you plan.

Similarly, you will find ways to plan your growing space while working in your strengths. If you do not fully know which strengths to utilize, that's all right. Hopefully, by the end of this book you'll be able to reflect upon talents and skills that you either have or want to develop, and how you can best utilize them to build the garden you want. Also, since we're walking through this together, I will outline the types of garden options that exist. This may help with organizing designs and ideas for how to best build with the space that you have.

You do not need a large plot of land to create a productive green space. Balcony gardens allow you to grow various vegetables, fruits, herbs, and flowers within a small space. You are only limited by your imagination.

ORNAMENTAL VS. EDIBLE GARDENS

Your garden is a reflection of you—your personality, your preferences, and even your motivation. No matter who you are, the way you build your garden will represent your personality. You have the ability to make any space into a garden, whether with raised beds, pots, or simply the earth around you, but you'll need to decide the type of garden you want. Why is that a challenge? Because deciding on the type of garden you want can sometimes feel like going down a rabbit hole, especially if you're just beginning. If you have searched the internet, books, or even social media for ideas, you'll see a wide variety of options, which can be inspiring but also overwhelming. I will lay out a few options for your consideration, without throwing you into information overload. Although there are dozens of gardens to choose from, I'll spend this time highlighting two main types: ornamental and edible gardens. An ornamental garden is meticulously designed for aesthetic appeal and enjoyment, while an edible garden is for cultivating

food. There's much planning involved in both, but the types of plants that are grown and the way they are arranged differentiates the two even further.

A couple of years ago I visited the Sarah P. Duke Gardens in Durham, North Carolina, and I remember thinking how beautifully curated each specialized garden was. This garden is situated on 55 acres at Duke University and features four main botanical spaces, each with a distinct focus. I vividly remember two unique gardens: one that cultivated historic bulbs, ornamental grasses, shrubs, and heirloom roses, and another that showcased the rich floral diversity in Southeast Asia—Japanese maples, ginger lilies, peonies, and mosses. Both gardens were strategically landscaped with artistic themes. Yet, despite the careful planning that went into designing these gardens in the heart of the city, each complemented the surrounding environment and wildlife. Of course, extensive horticultural expertise was behind the construction of these breathtaking

Rudbeckia hirta, also known as black-eyed Susan, is a popular perennial wildflower grown in North America. With their bright color, they are guaranteed to bring cheer to any garden.

Zinnia elegans, or simply zinnia, provide pollinators with sweet nectar and make beautiful cut flowers for vases.

attractions; however, both spaces are representative of ornamental gardens.

Ornamental botanical spaces are generally seen in public spaces (after all, their function is for visual appeal), yet examples like the Sarah P. Duke Gardens are more formal examples. To be sure, ornamental gardens can be cultivated in your own backyard. The most common items in an ornamental garden, whether public or private, are flowers, foliage plants, trees, grasses, rocks, and even aquatic elements. The Duke Gardens emphasize how building an ornamental garden is an excellent way to show off any creative skills you may have, as it is an art form. How you choose to situate these items and get them to flourish is where the opportunity to create a masterpiece lies. Thankfully, there are many popular styles that may further inspire ideas for your own space, such as Zen, cottage, modern, and tropical aesthetics.

Now on to edible gardens, or gardens cultivated to produce food. When I lived in South Carolina, I observed my grandfather (whom I affectionately call "Papa") work on his garden every spring and summer. It wasn't intricately designed, nor were the

plants strategically placed. As a matter of fact, he simply tilled the ground and made plots where he desired to grow plants. He added fertilizers to create a nutrient-dense foundation, but his gardening regimen was fairly straightforward: regular watering, weed management, and pest control. South Carolina's subtropical climate, especially in the Pee Dee region, also provided near-perfect temperatures for growing specific vegetables and fruits. During the summer months I used to lightheartedly refer to the region as "a convection oven," with its days consisting of high humidity and temperatures reaching over 100°F (38°C). If you've been to South Carolina in the summer, you know exactly what I mean. But in this climate Papa was able to keep a modest, yet steady production of summer squash, cucumbers, and hot peppers. He lived simply, using what he had, to grow what was familiar to him, and though he did not use organic growing methods, his growing space was his pride and sharing his harvests with family and friends was his joy. You can say the apple didn't fall too far from the tree because I developed a similar pride and joy in gardening. It's also important to note that we lived in a deeply rural

Golden crookneck squash has always been a favorite vegetable to grow, as it reminds me of when my grandparents used to harvest the fruits to make a warm bowl of sautéed squash with Vidalia onions.

community, where access to nutritional food options posed a challenge. So, watching Papa take a seed and nurture it into a delicious consumable sparked something in me—a deep curiosity of "what if?" Through gardening, access to more food choices became evident.

The main function of edible gardens is for food production, and unlike ornamental gardens, these gardens are significantly more conscious of the local ecosystem. Earlier in this chapter I explained how organisms must collaborate for ecological balance to be maintained, and this concept is especially relevant when constructing edible gardens. But why? Common consumable plants include edible flowers, herbs, edible shrubs, vegetables, and fruits. Most, if not all, require a joint effort with other organisms to properly develop and produce. For instance, edible flowers not only provide food for humans, but they also attract and provide food for pollinators, and these same pollinators assist with fertilizing many vegetable and fruit plants. Similarly, herbs not only make medicinal elixirs and delicious culinary seasonings, but also serve as a repellent to unwanted pests.

Though there are clear definitions and purposes between the two types of gardens, I'm going to blur the lines a bit: You are actually not limited to choosing one or the other. With creative design and planning, these two types of gardens may be interplanted or included in a single space. Interplanting ornamentals, such as certain perennial and annual flowers, with edible plants fosters a harmonious environment and benefits the two types. For example, ornamental flowering bushes, like camellias, provide an abundance of nectar for honeybees and hummingbirds, so introducing this plant will encourage beneficial organisms into your garden. Lavender plants add a cheery pop of color to your space, and because of their strong aroma, they are frequently used in borders to repel deer and rabbits.

If you haven't noticed by now, edible gardens compare to ornamental gardens in that they too require a bit of strategizing and proactive planning. It is important to be mindful of the types of plants you seek to grow, their arrangement in your designated space, and the timing in which they are planted. It takes a bit of research and artistry to construct and maintain a garden that produces optimally, but it's utilizing this type of creativity that is one of the best aspects of being a gardener.

Pollinator houses and beehives provide shelter and a safe space for pollinating insects to live and raise their young.

The fragrant lavender plant undoubtedly has many benefits for humans, but it is also a protective companion to other plants and food for pollinators.
Next page: You can create your space to be whatever you desire, but it doesn't have to happen overnight. Building a garden is truly a labor of love and patience.

SEVEN GARDENING METHODS

There are many gardening methods by which plants are cultivated in the following types of spaces. Each method serves a specific function and there are many reasons why one method may be preferred over another. It all depends upon the resources you have, what you're aiming to grow, and the frequency at which you hope to grow. The chart on page 31 features the advantages and disadvantages for the seven common garden methods we'll discuss here. Just as the types of gardens can be integrated together, various gardening methods can be utilized in one space as well. In our garden, we have implemented six out of the seven gardening methods in one space—you're not limited to just one. To help you understand the function and purpose of each method, I'll explain how we have made use of nearly all of them.

FLOWER GARDENS

Each year we allocate one raised bed for nurturing a variety of recommended native flowers, such as *Echinacea purpurea* (purple coneflower), *Monarda didyma* (bee balm), and *Asclepias tuberosa* (butterfly weed). Though we grow flowers all around the garden, the garden bed that we exclusively select for flowers is typically centralized so that it can be seen and accessed from all directions. My favorite characteristic of flower gardens is when the flowers are at peak bloom, as they add such vibrance to our space. Our flower bed always enhances the aesthetic of the garden with sweet aromas and various hues of purple, pink, red, and yellow. I frequently use flower petals in conjunction with herbs to make teas and balms. From spring to early autumn, we experience a diverse presence of insects and birds, and it is quite fascinating to watch them humming and chirping within the plants. We realized the importance of maintaining a flower garden to help sustain our native plant and pollinator populations. Flower gardens are multipurpose and carry countless benefits for you and the surrounding wildlife.

RAISED BED GARDENS

A raised bed is an elevated box that is filled with enough soil to support plants without using the soil underneath the box. Because of the height difference, many people find that this method of gardening is less strenuous on the back and provides greater protection against small animals that make their way into the garden. There are many types of materials that can be used to construct raised beds, including wood, galvanized steel, recycled plastics, and masonry. In our case, we opted for self-built beds made of lumber. Because the topography and soil on our property needed much work, we decided to use raised beds to offset the unlevel grading of our yard and to assist with water retention and drainage of our soil. On top of that, this gardening method gives us greater control over the quality of the soil and allows greater versatility in what we can grow. Though we must amend and top off the beds with new soil each season due to the occasional soil erosion, raised beds provide convenience and practicality that certainly make the costs worthwhile.

Flower gardens may be cultivated for obtaining flower decor, attracting pollinators, and creating an aesthetically pleasing landscape.

This 16-inch (40.6 cm) tall raised bed is made of wood. These types of beds are typically constructed with a height of at least 8 inches (20 cm).

A nontraditional and soilless way to grow plants and vegetables may be through a hydroponic system, which uses nutrient-rich aqueous solutions as the growing medium.

HYDROPONIC GARDENS

Hydroponic gardening is the only method that we have not implemented in our garden.

You may be wondering what exactly a hydroponic garden is. And if you have deduced that the prefix *hydro* means "water," then you are halfway to the answer. Hydroponic gardening is a soilless garden method where water and dissolved nutrients provide the medium for growing plants. This option is great for small spaces or for the gardener who lacks ground space for an outdoor garden. Depending on the complexity of the hydroponic system, the up-front costs may be more expensive, but there are many advantages to hydroponically growing plants, herbs, and even vegetables. Additionally, the need for pest, weed, and disease management significantly decreases because many of these issues are predominantly found in soil conditions. The foundational setup for this method usually involves a reservoir, a nutrient source, and, of course, water. Lastly, this approach typically requires electricity or some advanced technology for the system to operate, but many gardeners find hydroponically grown plants require less water and produce greater yields due to vital nutrients being readily available and easily accessible.

GREENHOUSE GARDENS

Because we enjoy growing vegetables year-round, our 10- by 12-foot (3 by 3.7 m) greenhouse allows us to extend our growing season and offers a more protected environment for some of our immature fruit trees and seedlings when the temperature drops. Greenhouses vary in size, where some can fit in small spaces, while others require professional assembly and large plots of land. In our first year of gardening, we used a small portable greenhouse kit to start all our seeds. We got a head start on the growing season and were able to protect the seedlings from sudden late frosts and pests. Depending on the size you obtain, regular maintenance may be required to ensure the quality of the greenhouse. For instance, temperature control and proper ventilation help prevent heat damage to plants and the occurrence of fungus. Though up-front costs may vary, I have found that greenhouses contribute greatly to the successful production of vegetables and fruits each year in our garden. Whichever size you choose, greenhouses provide a controlled environment for growing virtually anything.

Greenhouses not only provide an additional space for cultivating your plants but also extend your growing season.

VERTICAL GARDENS

Vertical gardens offer a unique alternative to growing horizontally and strictly on the ground, especially if space is a limiting factor. Due to their compact size, vertical gardens often make growing ornamental and edible plants possible for small spaces and even indoors. Whether you are constructing a do-it-yourself vertical growing space or purchasing a vertical gardening kit, there are many options for obtaining this aesthetic and the results are comparable to those of conventional methods. Moreover, they are quite simple to build and provide better ventilation for plants because they are positioned to receive greater airflow. Since these tend to not cover much surface area, frequent rotation of the garden is recommended to make sure each plant receives sufficient light. Tyler and I often use a portable vertical garden to grow herbs and small vegetables around the deck of our home. This area is not very large, so a vertical growing space keeps things tidy while giving us the ability to grow food right outside our door.

This portable vertical garden offers a convenient way to grow and display flowers, herbs, and smaller vegetables where space may be limited.

Container gardens offer much versatility in where and how you can grow edible and ornamental plants.

CONTAINER GARDENS

Container gardens are one of the easiest ways to start a garden. From my experience, container gardens possess the advantages of both raised beds and vertical gardens but are significantly more cost-efficient. They do not require much space and offer great versatility in terms of arrangement. Depending on your space, style, and the plants you hope to grow, containers like pots, bags, and even storage bins may be used for creating fun growing spaces. Container materials include terra-cotta, metal, plastic, wood, and concrete. Whatever material you use, it is important that it is durable and safe for growing consumables. Though this type of gardening method offers greater versatility in where you can cultivate plants, growing capacity is often limited.

In our second year of gardening, we experimented with growing tomatoes, peppers, leafy greens, and root vegetables in 18-gallon storage bins, simply for the convenience of quickly expanding our space. To successfully grow vegetables in containers, seasonal soil replacements and considerably more water were required, but we received bountiful harvests throughout the year.

IN-GROUND GARDENS

For many, in-ground gardens can be significantly less expensive than garden beds, and depending on your garden's location and soil type, tilling and amending the soil may be the only preparation required. For starters, selecting a suitable location that is sufficiently ventilated, receives at least six to eight hours of full sun, and possesses well-draining, nutrient-rich soil mix will be key to producing vigorous edible and ornamental plants. One major benefit to in-ground gardening is the ability to customize the foundation to any size that your space allows.

Though most of our garden comprises raised beds, we enjoy growing some of the larger vegetables such as corn, squash, and beans directly in the ground. Regular maintenance is strongly recommended, as in-ground gardens are more prone to weeds and pests, but with consistent upkeep, these challenges are reduced. Furthermore, installing a drip line ensures that each plant receives the water and nutrients it needs for maximum growth.

With a bit of tilling and soil amending, the in-ground garden is a quick and easy option. We opted to grow our corn, squash, and beans here this year.

ADVANTAGES AND DISADVANTAGES OF GARDENING METHODS

GARDENING METHOD	ADVANTAGES	DISADVANTAGES
Flower gardens	• Restores and preserves wildlife • Increases aesthetic appeal • Able to consume some types and make floral arrangements	• Not all flowers may be well suited to your locale • Involves extensive planning • May attract various insects
Raised bed gardens	• Loose soil with better drainage • Offers protection against small animals • Less strenuous on your back	• Expensive initial costs • Requires topping off soil each season • Limited growing space
Hydroponic gardens	• More water-efficient • Requires less space • No weeds	• Requires more light • Expensive setup costs • Reliant on advanced technology and electricity
Greenhouse gardens	• Provides a controlled growing environment • Able to grow year-round • Greater weed, pest, and disease control	• Higher operating costs • Requires regular maintenance • Expensive up-front costs
Vertical gardens	• Can build your own or purchase • Ideal for small spaces • Better ventilation	• Limited to shallow-rooted or vining plants • Requires frequent watering and fertilizing • May block sunlight for some plants
Container gardens	• Offers better protection against pests • Minimizes weeds • Fits smaller spaces	• Limited growing capacity • Requires more frequent watering • Requires soil replacement each year
In-ground gardens	• Growing space of any size • More cost-efficient • May not require soil purchase	• Requires soil tilling and amending • Higher likelihood of weeds • Requires large amount of space

A vibrant bowl of vegetables harvested at peak ripeness.

WHAT DOES THE GARDEN GIVE?

By now you can probably see how the garden provides holistic returns. When I started on my journey to becoming a gardener, I could not fathom the magnitude of tangible and intangible benefits that I would gain along the way. The production of diverse foods has been one advantage, but the character building has been an unexpected but welcomed opportunity. Apart from the fact that gardening serves as a healthy outlet and a means to get consistent exercise and mindfulness practices, there is scientific evidence that proves the value that gardens bring. On an individual level, studies have shown that gardening has been linked to improvements in health and well-being by increasing serotonin (the mood-stabilizing hormone) and decreasing cortisol (the primary stress hormone) in the brain. I can certainly attest to this because there's nothing like walking into a tranquil space surrounded by natural elements after a long and trying workday. On a societal level, gardens can improve access to higher-quality foods, promote greater physical activity, and strengthen community relationships. Though the above points outline the importance of gardens, I can't help but wonder, what is a garden without a gardener?

WHY ARE YOU (THE GARDENER) IMPORTANT?

If you were to ask a gardener why they are important, you're obviously not going to get a straight answer, as it's a difficult question to respond to. However, if you were to ask that same gardener what role they play in their communities or within the environment, you may be surprised to hear a common theme: stewardship. Stewardship is defined as the careful and responsible management of something. In this matter, that something may be the things in nature. Many gardeners feel a moral obligation to enhance the wellness of their communities and the environment. Within the community, gardeners tend to serve as stewards of the people, where they seek to educate and guide others on greater awareness of how plants impact the condition and health of society. Within the environment, gardeners serve as land stewards who seek to protect biodiversity and promote greater ecological sustainability. This sounds like a huge undertaking, but this type of care

Certifying your space as a wildlife habitat simply displays your commitment to being a mindful steward of the habitat around you.

isn't just a onetime occurrence; it is a consistent and gradual behavior that happens over time. You too may witness a gradual shift within yourself toward greater community and environmental stewardship. These incremental changes may also empower you to become a better steward of yourself, beginning with the quality of foods that you consume.

Gardens can provide nourishment for the body and an outlet to clear your mind.

THE JOURNEY TO BECOMING A GARDENER

One of the most fascinating facts that you may learn on your journey to becoming a gardener is what the act of gardening pulls out of you. In the road map on the next page, I have proposed seven defined moments that you may find yourself experiencing. In these moments I encourage you to stop and smell the roses, while reflecting upon where you are in your journey and how far you've come in your development.

1. IDENTIFYING YOUR WHY
What are your intrinsic motivations for gardening? What drives you to start? Sometimes your reasons may be rooted in past experiences or a desire to create greater impact. There's no right or wrong answer, and it can be as simple or complex as you like. This is your adventure and establishing your "why" is the fuel that will keep you going.

2. VISUALIZING YOUR POTENTIAL
Regardless of your experience level, visualizing the type of gardener that you aspire to be is an important exercise in your gardening evolution. There is a profound quote that says "you can't be what you can't see." Imagining the attributes that you hope to gain, and the gardening goals you hope to accomplish, will mentally prepare you for where you're going, helping you turn potentiality into actuality.

3. OVERCOMING THE CHALLENGES
In gardening, challenges may manifest themselves as losses, barriers, disappointments, and even fears. But one thing is sure: You will learn that you are stronger and braver than you thought. And it is in this place that you may find yourself capable of doing things that you did not realize you could do. Harnessing your "why" to propel you through challenges also cultivates resilience.

4. ACCEPTING THE UNCONTROLLABLE
Recognizing and accepting that some things are out of your control is tough, but humans did not create nature. We can foster elements of nature, but we are not the creators of it, so there are limitations in what we have control over. Humbling thought, no? You may realize that a gardener is a steward and not an owner of nature. Accepting that you are unable to control things not only promotes compassion but also facilitates a more peaceful and enjoyable gardening experience.

5. EMBRACING LEARNING OPPORTUNITIES

Every step of this journey is an opportunity to learn something new or expand upon what you already know. Gardens provide dynamic learning environments that engage all the senses. There is much to see, taste, touch, and smell. This lays the foundation for researching and exploring new topics and best practices. You may even make new gardening friends, which is not difficult to do.

6. EMPOWERING YOURSELF TO GROW

At some point you recognize the things that you can control, whether it is the health of yourself, those you love, or those in your community, and you are motivated to make a change. Whether you are gardening to produce food or as a hobby, empowerment comes when you're able to transform your intentions into actions. The time it took to get here does not matter. You are a gardener.

7. ENCOURAGING OTHERS TO BEGIN

You have gained so much on this path, learning more about yourself and the world around you. You have sowed seeds of persistence, overcome adverse moments, and successfully cultivated the garden you envisioned. In this place I am reminded of *Sankofa*, a term originating in Ghana that means "Go back and get it." Looking over your own progress as a gardener, remember where you came from, reach back and pull forth lessons that you have learned along the way, and inspire someone else to begin their own journey of becoming a gardener.

THE JOURNEY TO BECOMING A GARDENER

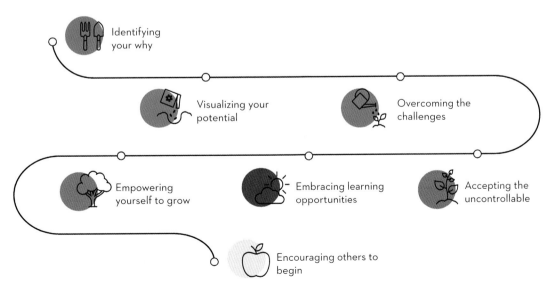

Identifying your why

Visualizing your potential

Overcoming the challenges

Empowering yourself to grow

Embracing learning opportunities

Accepting the uncontrollable

Encouraging others to begin

An early spring harvest basket of crisp greens, freshly picked squash, corn, and root vegetables.

Tomatoes are not only popular across many cultures, but these fruits have become significant staple food items globally.

CHAPTER 2

CREATING YOUR FOOD SECURITY

Gardens as a Resilient Intervention

WHAT IS FOOD SECURITY?

The universally accepted definition of food security describes "a state in which all people, at all times, have physical and economic access to sufficient, safe, and nutritious food to meet their dietary needs and food preferences for an active, healthy life." This is a powerful definition because it considers three simple yet crucial factors: each person, what they need, and how they can get what they need. The ability to obtain quality foods may unfortunately be influenced by many determinants, namely: affordability, availability, accessibility, and cultural appropriateness. It's apparent that exorbitant prices influence affordability on some of the healthier food options, especially in vulnerable low-income communities. Additionally, lack of consistent transportation and distance from nutritious food supplies significantly impact food availability. The last factor that is often overlooked is the cultural appropriateness of the food choices that are available.

Edible gardens help fill the nutritional gaps often found in food-insecure areas, while providing greater food selections.

Food patterns and preferences often vary from one culture to the next. These patterns are defined by what, how, and when food should be eaten according to an individual's culture. The concept of cultural appropriateness adds to the complexity of the food access dynamic, as dietary preferences relate to satisfaction and thereby influence whether a person will eat what is best for their health. This problem is not just reflective in the United States, but globally as well. And to go a step further, this issue is compounded in vulnerable and underrepresented communities. When any of the essential needs highlighted above are disrupted, acute and even chronic food insecurity may occur. To what degree it happens varies depending on physical, social, and economic status.

Every human around the globe needs to eat; food is the basis for survival. Yet the term "food" has many definitions, one being any substance consumed to provide support for an organism. Such a simple definition can further complicate gauging whether a person is receiving the nourishment they need regularly. However, the food security conversation shines a light on the fact that food is more than just a substance. Not only is eating food important for survival, but the quality and types of food people eat may influence their ability to thrive as individuals and as a population. Now, I must pause and remind you that I am not a dietitian, and nor will I pretend to be one for this book. I am only seeking to highlight my learned experience and the research that has been done by scientists, nutrition professionals, and medical providers to understand the relationship between food security and its impact on our health. In a few moments, there will be some scientific jargon that may or may not be familiar to you; however, it will be rather short and is something that we can all relate to.

Globally, the impact of food insecurity is shown to be related to the prevalence of, or likelihood of developing, chronic diseases. There is growing evidence that diet plays a significant role in the development

Gardening may not be the solution that ends all of global food insecurity, but it can put households on a path to being less reliant on commercial producers for all of their food options.

of some chronic diseases such as cancer, heart disease, type 2 diabetes, hypertension, stroke, and obesity. Many research studies have shown that poor nutritional intake has been steadily on the rise for many multidimensional reasons, ranging from biological and environmental issues to limitations in food access. A recent report in *The State of Food Security in the World*, showed that nearly 750 million people are affected by severe food insecurity and approximately two billion people lack access to safe, nutritious, and sufficient food. So, what does this mean? The dimensions of food security and disease burden are intersectional, and without sustainable food strategies, this global issue will continue to grow. This may sound daunting, but this is where I believe growing your own food may come into play.

In the introduction, I told you about the few years I spent in rural South Carolina, and how I personally experienced challenges with food security. At the time, my grandparents and I lived deep in the country, where the nearest grocery store was about

a thirty-minute drive away. The next description will sound like an exaggerated rural scene from a movie, but I promise you it is not. The town had one blinking traffic light and a small corner gas station that doubled as a convenient food shop. The items sold were processed items, such as chips, sodas, and packaged sweet cakes. The kitchen prepared meals, like pies, fries, fried chicken, bacon, grits, and other southern delicacies. Most of these items were high in sodium, sugar, and saturated and trans fats, but they were satisfying and filling to those who consumed them—and perhaps those who had no other option but to consume them.

As time passed, the town gained its first chain store, a small-box discount retailer. If you are not familiar with these types of stores, they offer affordable consumables and household items, but often lack healthier, nutritionally balanced food options, as processed lower-nutrient food items are more common and have a longer shelf life. Now, I would be remiss if I did not add how consumer preferences impact what is supplied in stores. Because markets are driven by the demand of consumers, dietary preferences also influence whether stores and local markets can even afford to consistently supply more nutritious options.

Nonetheless, imagine living in a rural community and these types of consumable items are predominantly available and accessible to you each day; this type of diet is bound to impact your health in some way, right? Well, as a matter of fact, there is statistical data that supports the notion that people in rural communities are at a higher risk for chronic diseases compared to residents in urban communities, and these statistics are reflected in various rural communities around the globe. Therefore, it is unfortunate but not a surprise that over time, health challenges and the occurrence of chronic diseases are exactly what happened to me, my grandparents, and many other members of my community. Diet-related diseases and high mortality rates were and still are all too common in towns like where I lived. Each year, nearly 41 million people from all over the world die from chronic diseases. So, when you experience or see the effects of food insecurity one too many times, it ignites you to make a change. And fortunately, just as your health can decline due to diet, it is possible for it to also improve due to diet.

Though I described how food insecurity may be presented in a specific rural community, this crisis is not limited to just rural areas, as it is also evident in urban areas and on a global scale. The face of food security can vary from one community to the next, but what makes this such a multidimensional issue is that there are varying disparities that exist. For instance, rural and urban communities have occasional overlap with their barriers, yet the structural, economic, and cultural burdens between the two differ significantly. The vast differences between the infrastructure in rural communities compared to urban areas often affect proximity and transportation to larger food supply chains with healthier food options. Moreover, the nearby stores that are present are typically small convenient stores that either do not carry fresh and nutritious food items or have low variety, similar to the corner gas station that I described.

I have emphasized the spectrum of food security as it pertains to different communities, but there is an interesting dynamic at play, where lack of proper nutrition is seen in both states of poverty and wealth. Peculiar, right? It's easier to comprehend the nutritional disparities within those who are experiencing any degree of poverty, but disparities present in those who possess greater wealth are equally troubling. This may be a bit of a surprise, but wealth does not automatically equate to greater food security. More wealth may increase access and provide the means to afford healthier options, but wealth does not always lead to the best nutritional choices, especially when suboptimal options are in abundance. Examples of these are called food swamps, or environments saturated with a surplus of nutritionally unhealthy options. Given, evidence shows that food swamps are more likely to be located in lower-income communities. But one thing is sure: Correlation does not always imply causation. The bottom line is that there are many food options that are lacking the balanced nutrition people need to thrive, and an over-reliance on them can have negative health effects. Consequently, there are a lot of people eating consistent meals, but technically still experiencing hunger because they are not receiving the nutrients that their bodies need.

Cucumber plants are prolific producers and their nutritious and crisp fruits can be prepared in a variety of ways, including raw.

Homemade juices using fresh produce are another way to consume the nutritious goodness growing in your garden.

An array of brightly colored food options expands what you can create in your meals, thus giving you access to greater nourishment.

In summary, there are simply not enough healthy food options to consistently feed everyone in many communities around the world. And there is much more work to be done in the fight to create more robust strategies for combating food insecurity. Despite illuminating the challenges of food security, I wouldn't dare take you down into the problem without lifting you to a possible solution—after all, that's where hope and empowerment lie. Growing your own food through a garden can serve as an integral strategy to enhance your diet and improve your own food security. So, if you can, visualize taking a bit more control of your well-being through growing wholesome nourishment in whatever space you have. That alone is liberating in more aspects than one.

Tomatoes and cucumbers produce in abundance and make a great summer snack or side dish.

Opposite: The road to greater food security can start with the fruits in your garden.

THE TERMS

There are many terms frequently used in discussions on food security, but not all are truly understood. Below, I have included some helpful words and definitions to know in the food security conversation.

Food security	A situation where all people, at all times, have physical and economic access to sufficient, safe, and nutritious food to meet their dietary needs and food preferences for an active, healthy life (Committee on World Food Security)
Food insecurity	A situation that exists when people lack secure access to sufficient amounts of safe and nutritious food for normal growth and development and an active and healthy life (Food and Agriculture Organization)
Food access	Access by individuals to adequate resources (entitlements) for acquiring appropriate foods for a nutritious diet (Committee on World Food Security)
Food equity	The concept that all people have the ability and opportunity to grow and consume healthful, affordable, and culturally significant foods (University at Buffalo, Global Health Equity)
Food desert	Areas where people have limited access to a variety of healthy and affordable food (USDA)
Food swamp	Environments saturated with unhealthy foods because of the large numbers of corner stores and fast-food outlets in them (CDC)
Food sovereignty	The right of people to healthy and culturally appropriate food produced through ecologically sound and sustainable methods, and their right to define their own food and agriculture systems (La Via Campesina)

Imagine walking out to your garden to harvest fresh vegetables, like this eggplant, for your meal.

GARDENS AS AN INTERVENTION TO FOOD ACCESS

Now that we have discussed the data around food security, let's look at how the gardener and the act of gardening help fill in the gap. By now it may be evident that growing your own food can afford you access to not just greater food, but also more nutritious and culturally relevant food options. Yet, one point that is often overlooked is that anyone—no matter their financial circumstance, their background, or their experience with plants (or lack thereof)—can learn to grow food and secure greater food options than what is commercially presented. So, you may be asking, how could gardening directly improve or enhance food security for yourself and others? Allow me to guide you through three possible ways.

The first way that gardening can enhance food security is by offering greater diversity in your produce options. Also, eating more diverse food may increase your ability to take in more essential micro- and macronutrients. This promotes a more nutrient-dense diet. There are thousands of vegetables and fruits available for you to grow and consume, and the mere act of gardening encourages you to explore and experiment with many of these selections. Now, I must confess that it isn't easy to peruse a catalog with so many interesting and mouthwatering seed options and choose what you need for growing each season. However, the fact that these options exist can stir a sense of excitement.

The second way that gardening can enhance food security is by providing savings on the cost of food and the potential for generating income. It is an unfortunate reality that in many places, the cost of fresh commercially available produce is significantly higher than some of the more processed and less nutritional foods. Also, there are many factors like production, manufacturing, and transportation logistics that contribute to the costs of commercially sold produce. Growing your own food allows you to

You can grow food from hundreds of varieties of vegetable, fruit, and herb seeds, which can also give you access to foods not commonly found in stores.

Freshly picked garden fruits, like strawberries, can be made into decadent treats like homemade jam. They can even be produced for selling at your local farmers' market.

omit many of the processes that food undergoes to get to you, and it lets you experience greater quality because the food is able to move from the ground to your table in less time. Cultivating a garden may also inspire you to create garden products that can be used to seek entrepreneurial opportunities.

The third and last way that gardening can enhance food security is by helping you be prepared for unexpected changes to your access to certain foods. There are many economical, biological, and social reasons as to why access to food could be limited; however, the intention of this book is to not focus on what is out of your control, but to simply refocus on what may be within your control. I previously highlighted how maintaining an edible garden can result in an abundance of fresh food. As it happens, this abundance can be preserved for later consumption using methods such as canning, dehydrating, and freezing. Preserving your garden harvests will allow you to enjoy more food options no matter the season or any circumstance beyond your control.

That said, it may be a bit naive to assume that maintaining a garden will solve the full magnitude of food insecurity in the world. Nevertheless, gardens may help alleviate the nutritional gaps that are common in households around the world, making it possible to access consistently healthier, home-grown alternatives. Gardening allows you to grow a wide variety of produce that may be quite costly in supermarkets. Each year, Tyler and I grow nearly a dozen cultivars of heirloom tomatoes and several varieties of peppers, squash, peas, and beets. Because of this, we significantly cut the costs of produce purchases, and depending on the types of vegetables and plants you grow in your edible garden, you may not even see some of these items readily available in commercial stores. An added benefit to growing your own food is having the ability to diversify your diet with healthier, nutrient-rich fresh foods. The freshness of food is also key, as much of the produce sold in grocery stores undergoes lengthy processes from the time of harvest to distribution.

When the garden produces an abundance of food, preserving surplus produce through canning is a great way to reduce waste and keep healthy food options accessible year-round.

TAKING CONTROL OF WHAT ENTERS OUR BODIES

As we've journeyed along, I have frequently recited and emphasized the power that food possesses, especially when it enters our bodies. Food is life, and food provides the fuel for our mind and body to grow and flourish. But it's important to remember that not everything may technically be considered good food, and to be more specific, not everything may be considered good food for you. The types and quality of food that you consume can positively or negatively affect your health and overall wellness. Access to better-quality foods increases the likelihood and opportunity for you to consume more nutritious options. There is an additional dynamic at play that involves food that is best for your cultural and dietary needs. Examples of such cultural considerations include place of origin, race, age, economic situation, and religion, and each of these can influence the types of foods you gravitate toward or away from. Therefore, being able to consistently acquire the types of foods you need to function optimally gives you greater control over what enters your body. Luckily, growing your own food allows you to create the opportunity for yourself.

I want to remind you that I am not here to make recommendations on what you should and shouldn't eat; that is not my domain of expertise. However, it is my hope to inspire you to reflect upon food options that may not be readily available—options that you have the ability to produce through your very own hands. I don't think many medical experts would argue with the idea that many of us can be a bit more mindful of what enters our bodies. From personal experience, cultivating an edible garden has given me greater control over how to grow the food that I desire to eat and feed my family. I opt for cultivating the plants in my garden using organic products and methods, which means that all products and materials are derived directly from minerals, animals, and plants. There are many ecological reasons for this preference, such as minimizing soil erosion, encouraging biodiversity, and protecting the water supply, but a major reason is to minimize unnecessary exposure to potentially harmful synthetic pesticides, herbicides, and fertilizers. This helps ensure that what I consume is the best quality of produce and there are no residual harmful substances that can disrupt my health and the health of the surrounding ecosystem. After all, we are also organisms within that ecosystem.

While I don't cast judgment on how someone sets out on their food-growing path (because there are numerous ways to get started), it does bring me great joy to guide and encourage others in how to select the best plants and growing methods for the types of foods they are seeking to grow. As gardeners, if we want to inspire and motivate others to garden and grow their own food, then we have to be willing to educate with gentleness and encourage with empathy, even if the techniques and methods that are used may not be what we perceive is best. I am reminded of the saying "If you knew better, you would do better," which simply means that if you had sufficient knowledge and ability, you would almost

Okra is a summer staple in many regions, especially the southeastern United States. Some people like them mixed with other ingredients, but I think they are just perfect when cooked by themselves.

feel compelled to make a better choice. I appreciate this saying because it has automatically built in some limitations here; you don't have to do things perfectly or best, just better. And perhaps this is the way we can view the journey of growing and consuming healthier food options.

The path to food sovereignty through growing your own food is a holistic journey that consists of empowerment, education, and encouragement. But how can gardens and growing your own food build greater resilience? That is the topic of the next section.

Opposite: Edible bliss is cracking open a fresh cantaloupe straight off the vine and enjoying it at its peak ripeness.

Being mindful of your food-growing methods helps you be a more conscious gardener. You can also trust that the food you consume will be good for you.

As you're starting out, strive to grow items that you frequently eat. For my household, a few of these items are heirloom tomatoes and peppers.

Growing food in your own space offers the convenience of hand selecting exactly what you need, when you need it.

GARDENS AS A SYMBOL OF RESILIENCE

There has been a lot of talk in recent years about how gardens serve as a beacon of hope and resilience, especially during times of economic hardships, societal tension, and public health crises. These types of pressures typically inspire people to reflect upon their well-being, whether it be through nutrition, work-life balance, or even mental health. If you've been paying attention to current events, you may have even noticed the increasing interest in gardening over the past few years. People are seeking greater balance in life, less stress, and better-quality food, and it just so happens that gardening provides a solution for all of these. Whether you are doing it for sport or for survival, gardening has the ability to impact your life, and in a good way.

What does the term "resilience" mean, and how does it relate to gardening? Resilience is the capacity to bounce back or recover from a challenge. When I think of the word "resilience," I am reminded of the fruit fly, or *Drosophila melanogaster*, a common garden and home pest. Not only do they reproduce quickly, but they are also fast movers and you are guaranteed to miss if you swat at them. And if, by chance, you do make contact, they bounce up as if nothing ever happened. Fruit flies have the ability to survive and thrive by any means necessary. These insects will find ways to access the food and shelter they need, whether that be under floor mats, in drains, around garden beds, or near compost. Now, I recognize that this may be a bit oversimplified, as there is a lot that goes into building resilience for a human, but I mention the fruit fly example to highlight a lesson that applies to you and me: Cultivating a garden provides us with opportunities to grow what we need to survive and thrive—and by any means necessary.

The garden also serves as a symbol of resilience. I've often heard people speak about the need to start edible gardens to prepare for a moment when the local and global food supply may be compromised or unstable, and this can indeed happen. However, being a resilient gardener doesn't mean that you have to intensively garden and store away years' worth of food as you await impending doom (although there is nothing wrong with doing so if you have the time, resources, and motivation). Gardening promotes resilience in a much more balanced way. It's easy to go down the rabbit hole of hypothetical events that could possibly occur. There are many types of catastrophes that we could plan for, but in the end, most are unforeseen. Gardening helps you focus on improving the state that you are in today and in the very near future as well. Thus, a great balanced activity may be to grow a steady rotation of staple crops, which are the foods that are a major part of your diet and supply most of your energy and nutrient needs from day to day, such as corn, potatoes, beans, and grains. This will ultimately provide you with the chance to indulge in the foods you need in the present, while gradually preparing for what you may need in the future.

If an event were to occur that disrupted your food supply—say a gradual one, like your area developed into a food swamp—you would have the ability to nutritionally adjust or recover more easily due to the foods that you have produced in your garden. Therefore, gardening encourages you to be like the fruit fly; whatever challenges or barriers that may pop up will not permanently disrupt your ability to

Sweet potatoes are root vegetables high in fiber and essential vitamins and minerals, and serve as great staple crops.

eat what is good for you. This is the nature of true resilience that can be fostered through the development of an essential life skill, which is gardening and growing your own food.

Opposite: As a gardener, you have the right to define your own food and the ability to grow it through ecologically sound ways.

PERSPECTIVES OF A GARDENER

Meet Jasmine Jefferson
Location: Florida
Social Media Handle: @blackgirlswithgardens
Website: blackgirlswithgardens.com

MY GARDENING JOURNEY

I've been gardening for nearly seven years now, and it's been such an enlightening journey, to say the least. The best way to describe my gardening journey is dimensional and restorative. During this process, I've learned much about myself and I'm not sure I would have discovered many of these things outside of gardening. I find so much joy and peace in growing and sharing food, and guiding others on how to grow their own food. And of course the gardening community has contributed to the enjoyment of this journey in a major way.

Jasmine in front of her Florida garden holding a bunch of celery.

MOTIVATION TO BEGIN

I started gardening after my maternal grandmother passed away. I took over caring for her plants, and after a successful six months of caring for one of her aloe vera plants, I sought to grow herbs, vegetables, and flowers. At that point, I explored growing something new each season. While I experienced many garden successes and failures, each motivated me to experiment with different methods in order to learn more. And those lessons propelled me forward.

Jasmine uses a mix of raised and vertical beds to grow fresh produce for her family nearly year-round.

EDIBLE GARDENING AND FOOD SOVEREIGNTY

Becoming a gardener has empowered me to take control of what my family and I consume. Gardening started as a hobby, but as I learned more about sustainable gardening practices such as soil health, optimal fertilizers, and composting techniques, it became clear that I (and others as well) needed greater authority over not only the types of food we eat, but also the quality of those foods. Gardening has taught me that we all have a place in agriculture if we wish to explore it. Whether you are a flower farmer, medicine/herb grower, or the scientist studying our soil composition, you can find your lane (or create one) by cultivating good food for your community.

HOW GARDENING INFLUENCES MY PERSPECTIVE ON FOOD AND THE ENVIRONMENT

Gardening awoke an appreciation of food that I allow in my body. I've also come to realize that food and gardening are deeply connected to our cultural identity. How we cultivate the land and grow food that is good for us is intertwined in who we are. I believe, somehow and at some point, we have gotten away from that. Many of our ancestors encouraged growing food and practiced gardening methods that complemented healthy lifestyles and regenerative agriculture well before they became buzzwords. This cultural identity is at the forefront of my mind when I think of the term "good food."

Futhermore, to cultivate a healthy garden, you need a healthy ecosystem where every necessary component can thrive. I view my community in a similar way—as an ecosystem. In 2017, I founded Black Girls with Gardens, an organization that aims to provide representation, inspiration, support, and education to women of color exploring gardening. Through this platform, we guide women of color with tips and resources on how to connect with their cultural identity through gardening and growing their own food. It is my philosophy that we must learn how to heal our ecosystem (our communities) in order to combat some of the environmental, social, and economical challenges that we, as humans, encounter. And I have found that gardening has been an effective intervention for doing just that.

EMPOWERED TO GROW NEW FOODS

I'm pretty sure that I may have never tried cauliflower, eggplant, zucchini, yellow squash, or Brussels sprouts if I never grew them. To this day, I am amazed at how limited my vegetable intake was prior to starting my own garden. Since starting my gardening journey, I have studied hundreds of plants, vegetables, and herbs and their medicinal properties. And now, 25 to 30 percent of my garden is dedicated to growing and trying new varieties of vegetables and herbs. So, gardening has introduced me to an entirely new realm of wellness, and it's the most empowered I've felt in my life.

A handmade sweetgrass basket holding a summer harvest of various peppers and cherry tomatoes from Jasmine's subtropical garden.

CHAPTER 3

GETTING DOWN AND DIRTY

Starting Your Garden and Overcoming the Challenges

Previously we walked through the types of garden options that you may consider when starting your garden. It's also important to add that you do not have to permanently commit to one type of garden; you can explore and cultivate any type of garden at any point in your journey. I actually recommend you do just that so you can find the methods that work best for you. Now, you have seen that there are many types of gardens to choose from, but since we are talking about food in this book, we will be focusing on steps to take and things you will need to construct an edible garden. As we move forward, I'll detail a few topics for you to consider, such as space, resources, equipment, and vision. So, how do you begin from where you are and with what you have?

Opposite: Growing up, I associated soil with something to avoid coming into contact with. Since gardening, I have realized that soil is the medium for growth, and I am no longer afraid of getting dirty.

This garden bed produces more than fifty aromatic and healing herbs that we commonly use in our foods and tinctures.

SPACE

Gardens come in many shapes and sizes, and no matter what space you have available, building an edible garden is possible. As highlighted in chapter 1, one of the first and most things to do is examine an area that you are considering as a growing space. Most vegetable and fruit plants need full sunlight for an average of six to eight hours per day, so you want to make sure your area receives ample light. Not everyone has access to outdoor growing spaces, but luckily there are full-spectrum LED grow lights that you can use so that your plants get the light they need to photosynthesize.

In addition to light, growing capacity and proper ventilation will be keys to consider in selecting a growing space. As most edible plants grow, they develop below- and aboveground systems, or roots and shoots; both of these require room to spread in order for the plant to grow productively. An area that is properly ventilated or able to receive consistent airflow is necessary for reducing diseases and promoting strong plant limbs. Understanding the space you have will determine what will grow best. I have provided a handy "Edible Plants Gardening" chart that includes tips on spacing, ideal temperatures, and plants that grow well and don't grow well together. This chart may help as you consider the various plants you can grow in your garden.

EDIBLE PLANTS GARDENING

PLANTS	IDEAL TEMPERATURES FOR PLANTING	SPACING	GOOD COMPANIONS	BAD COMPANIONS
Arugula *Eruca vesicaria* ssp. *sativa*	40°F–53°F (5°C–12°C)	8–14 inches (20–35.6 cm)	Beans, beets, carrots, cucumbers, spinach, lettuce	Eggplant, tomatoes, peppers, potatoes
Asparagus *Asparagus officinalis*	75°F–85°F (24°C–30°C)	8–14 inches (20–35.6 cm)	Calendula, tomatoes	Onions, garlic
Basil *Ocimum basilicum*	50°F–70°F (10°C–21°C)	10–12 inches (25–30.5 cm)	Oregano, peppers, tomatoes, lettuce	Cucumbers, cabbage, cauliflower, rue, sage, rosemary
Beans (bush) *Phaseolus vulgaris*	70°F–90°F (21°C–32°C)	3–4 inches (7.5–10 cm)	Peas, radish, cucumbers, beets	Onions
Beans (pole) *Phaseolus vulgaris*	70°F–90°F (21°C–32°C)	4–6 inches (10–15 cm)	Carrots, corn, cucumbers, eggplant	Beets, onions
Beets *Beta vulgaris*	50°F–80°F (10°C–27°C)	8–12 inches (20–30.5 cm)	Bush beans, cabbage, onions, sage	None
Broccoli *Brassica oleracea* var. *italica*	50°F–85°F (10°C–30°C)	18–24 inches (45.7–61 cm)	Beans, beets, carrots, chives, cucumbers, dill, garlic, lettuce, spinach, thyme	Peppers, squash, tomatoes
Brussels sprouts *Brassica oleracea* var. *gemmifera*	50°F–85°F (10°C–30°C)	24 inches (61 cm)	Beets, bush beans, carrots, celery, onions, peas	Broccoli, cabbage, eggplant, peppers
Cabbage *Brassica oleracea* var. *capitata*	50°F–85°F (10°C–30°C)	9–12 inches (23–30.5 cm)	Beans, beets, carrots, chives, cucumbers, dill, garlic, lettuce, spinach, thyme	Peppers, squash, tomatoes
Cantaloupe *Cucumis melo* var. *cantalupensis*	75°F–95°F (24°C–35°C)	36–42 inches (91–106.7 cm)	Corn, radishes	None
Carrots *Daucus carota*	45°F–85°F (7°C–30°C)	1–2 inches (2.5–5 cm)	Tomatoes, leeks, onions, rosemary, sage, chives	Dill, potatoes
Cauliflower *Brassica oleracea* var. *botrytis*	50°F–85°F (10°C–30°C)	18–24 inches (45.7–61 cm)	Beans, beets, carrots, chives, cucumbers, dill, garlic, lettuce, spinach, thyme	Peppers, squash, tomatoes
Celery *Apium graveolens*	60°F–75°F (16°C–24°C)	12–18 inches (30.5–45.7 cm)	Bush beans, cabbage, leeks, onions, tomatoes	Corn, potatoes

PLANTS	IDEAL TEMPERATURES FOR PLANTING	SPACING	GOOD COMPANIONS	BAD COMPANIONS
Chives *Allium schoenoprasum*	60°F–70°F (16°C–21°C)	8–12 inches (20–30.5 cm)	Tomatoes, carrots, broccoli, cabbage, eggplant, mustard, peppers, squash	Asparagus, beans, peas, spinach
Cilantro *Coriandrum sativum*	55°F–70°F (13°C–21°C)	2–3 inches (5–7.5 cm)	Basil, mint, yarrow	Lavender, thyme, rosemary, fennel
Collards *Brassica oleracea var. viridis*	45°F–85°F (7°C–30°C)	15–18 inches (38–45.7 cm)	Potatoes, celery, dill, chamomile, sage, thyme	Broccoli, kale, cauliflower
Corn *Zea mays*	60°F–80°F (16°C–27°C)	10–15 inches (25–38 cm)	Beans, cucumbers, dill, melons, parsley, peas, sage, squash, thyme	Tomatoes, cabbage
Cucumbers *Cucumis sativus*	65°F–75°F (18°C–24°C)	8–10 inches (20–25 cm)	Beans, cabbage, corn, dill, lettuce, peas, onions, peppers, tomatoes	Sage
Eggplant *Solanum melongena*	80°F–90°F (27°C–32°C)	18–24 inches (45.7–61 cm)	Beans, herbs, marigolds, tomatoes, peppers, spinach	None
Fennel *Foeniculum vulgare*	50°F–70°F (10°C–21°C)	4–12 inches (10–30.5 cm)	None	None
Garlic *Allium sativum*	55°F–70°F (13°C–21°C)	6–12 inches (15–30.5 cm)	Beets, cabbage, carrots, dill, lettuce, parsley, Swiss chard, spinach, tomatoes	Peas, beans, sage
Green onions *Allium fistulosum*	45°F–70°F (7°C–21°C)	1–2 inches (2.5–5 cm)	Beets, cabbage, carrots, dill, lettuce, parsley, Swiss chard, spinach, tomatoes	Peas, beans, sage
Kale *Brassica oleracea var. sabellica*	45°F–80°F (7°C–27°C)	12–18 inches (30.5–45.7 cm)	Beans, beets, carrots, chives, cucumbers, dill, garlic, lettuce, spinach, thyme	Peppers, squash, tomatoes
Kohlrabi *Brassica oleracea var. gongylodes*	65°F–75°F (18°C–24°C)	9–12 inches (23–30.5 cm)	Beets, celery, cucumbers, onions	Peppers, pole beans, tomatoes
Leeks *Allium ampeloprasum*	55°F–75°F (13°C–24°C)	4–6 inches (10–15 cm)	Cabbage, tomatoes, beets, lettuce, carrots	Onions, garlic

PLANTS	IDEAL TEMPERATURES FOR PLANTING	SPACING	GOOD COMPANIONS	BAD COMPANIONS
Lettuce *Lactuca sativa*	55°F–70°F (13°C–21°C)	10–12 inches (25–30.5 cm)	Beets, cabbage, carrots, cucumbers, dill, garlic, onions, radishes, sage, spinach, squash, tomatoes, thyme	None
Melons *Cucumis melo*	70°F–90°F (21°C–32°C)	48 inches (122 cm)	Corn, radishes	None
Mint *Mentha* spp.	55°F–70°F (13°C–21°C)	18–24 inches (45.7–61 cm)	Oregano, marigolds, carrots, cabbage, tomatoes	Lavender, rosemary, sage, thyme
Mustard greens *Brassica juncea*	50°F–75°F (10°C–24°C)	6–8 inches (15–20 cm)	Dill, fennel, mint, corn, peas	Sunflower, soybeans, beans
Onion (bulb) *Allium cepa*	55°F–75°F (13°C–24°C)	4–6 inches (10–15 cm)	Beets, cabbage, carrots, dill, lettuce, parsley, Swiss chard, spinach, tomatoes	Peas, beans, sage
Oregano *Origanum vulgare*	65°F–70°F (18°C–21°C)	18–24 inches (45.7–61 cm)	Basil, peppers, cabbage	None
Parsley *Petroselinum crispum*	45°F–75°F (7°C–24°C)	1–2 inches (2.5–5 cm)	Carrots, chives, corn, onions, peas, peppers, tomatoes, sage, thyme	None
Peas *Pisum sativum*	40°F–70°F (5°C–21°C)	2–3 inches (5–7.5 cm)	Beans, carrots, corn cucumbers, parsley, peppers, radishes, sage, spinach, squash, thyme	Chives, onion, garlic
Peppers (bell) *Capsicum annuum*	65°F–80°F (18°C–27°C)	18–24 inches (45.7–61 cm)	Basil, carrots, cucumbers, onions, oregano, parsley	Cabbage, beans
Peppers (cayenne) *Capsicum frutescens*	65°F–80°F (18°C–27°C)	14–18 inches (35.6–45.7 cm)	Basil, carrots, cucumbers, onions, oregano, parsley	Cabbage, beans
Potatoes *Solanum tuberosum*	65°F–80°F (18°C–27°C)	8–12 inches (20–30.5 cm)	Beans, cabbage, marigolds	Tomatoes
Pumpkins *Cucurbita moschata*	50°F–90°F (10°C–32°C)	60–72 inches (152.4–183 cm)	Corn, radishes	None
Radishes *Raphanus sativus*	60°F–65°F (16°C–18°C)	½–4 inches (1.3–10 cm)	Beans, cucumbers, lettuce, peas, squash, spinach	Potatoes, turnips
Rhubarb *Rheum rhabarbarum*	40°F–80°F (5°C–27°C)	36–48 inches (91–122 cm)	Kale, turnips, cabbage, broccoli, beans, onions, garlic	Melons, tomatoes, cucumber

PLANTS	IDEAL TEMPERATURES FOR PLANTING	SPACING	GOOD COMPANIONS	BAD COMPANIONS
Rosemary *Salvia rosmarinus*	48°F–68°F (9°C–20°C)	8–24 inches (20–61 cm)	Beans, cabbage, carrots, peppers, sage, thyme	None
Rutabagas *Brassica napus* (Napobrassica Group)	45°F–85°F (7°C–30°C)	6–8 inches (15–20 cm)	Cabbage, broccoli, turnips, Brussels sprouts	Tomatoes, pole beans
Sage *Salvia officinalis*	60°F–70°F (16°C–21°C)	24–36 inches (61–91 cm)	Carrots, broccoli, cauliflower, kale	Cucumbers, onions, garlic, shallots, chives
Shallots *Allium cepa aggregatum*	40°F–90°F (5°C–32°C)	6–8 inches (15–20 cm)	Beets, cabbage, carrots, chamomile, mint, sage, thyme	Beans, peas
Spinach *Spinacia oleracea*	40°F–70°F (5°C–21°C)	2–4 inches (5–10 cm)	Cabbage, cilantro, leeks, lettuce, peas, sage	None
Squash *Cucurbita*	70°F–90°F (21°C–32°C)	18–28 inches (45.7–71 cm)	Corn, lettuce, onions, marigolds, melons, peas, peppers	Cabbage
Swiss chard *Beta vulgaris*	40°F–95°F (5°C–35°C)	6–12 inches (15–30.5 cm)	Beans, cabbage, garlic, onions, peppers, sage, thyme	None
Tarragon *Artemisia dracunculus*	50°F–75°F (10°C–24°C)	18–24 inches (45.7–61 cm)	Eggplant, lemon balm, marigolds	None
Thyme *Thymus vulgaris*	65°F–85°F (18°C–30°C)	9–12 inches (23–30.5 cm)	Grows well with all plants	None
Tomatoes *Solanum lycopersicum*	55°F–85°F (13°C–30°C)	24–36 inches (61–91 cm)	Cabbage, carrots, celery, onions, mint	Potatoes, corn, fennel
Turnips *Brassica rapa* ssp. *rapa*	40°F–75°F (5°C–24°C)	2–4 inches (5–10 cm)	Squash, tomatoes, celery, cabbage, broccoli, Brussels sprouts	Beets, carrots, onions, potatoes
Watermelons *Citrullus lanatus*	65°F–95°F (18°C–35°C)	48 inches (122 cm)	Corn, radishes	None
Yams *Dioscorea*	65°F–95°F (18°C–35°C)	12 inches (30.5 cm)	Dill, oregano, cilantro, basil	Squash
Zucchini *Cucurbita pepo*	70°F–90°F (21°C–32°C)	24–36 inches (61–91 cm)	Corn, lettuce, onions, marigolds, melons, peas, peppers	Cabbage

RESOURCES

Ah yes, the second most important components to consider when building your edible garden are the resources you have available. Sorry to break it to you, but building a garden is not free and it does not happen overnight, hence two primary resources you will need are funding and time. These are often underestimated in the planning and execution phase of building a garden, but there are proactive ways to mitigate coming up short on both.

When scoping out what you want your garden to look like and what you hope to grow, there are a few items of cost, such as garden beds, soil, seeds, and fertilizers, that should be taken into consideration. Many of these items can be fairly affordable individually, but the larger the growing space, the more that is required and costs can add up quickly. A good rule of thumb is to figure out a budgeted amount for your garden beforehand and procure your supplies and build your space with that number in mind.

The next resource is far more intangible but high in value, and that is time. Remember, becoming a gardener is a long-distance race, not a sprint. Planning, building, and maintaining all require time and effort. Even the fun of harvesting requires time! However, like costs, the bigger the space, the more time you may need to spend to make sure your garden is healthy and productive. Of course, once you establish your routine, maintaining the garden becomes somewhat of a habit. Nonetheless, it's important to have realistic expectations of what lies ahead, especially when valuable resources are required. This will set you up for greater success.

The kale and lettuce seedlings that have been steadily growing in the greenhouse for nearly a month are ready for transplanting into the outside.

EQUIPMENT

Procuring a good set of garden tools and equipment allows you to efficiently build and maintain your garden.

It goes without saying that tools make hard work more efficient and a little less strenuous on the body. Can you imagine trying to dig through compacted soil with your bare fingers? Yikes. I tried it once, and it didn't work out well—not a surprise. There are many tools with specific functions that are essential for the tasks required in the garden, and they may keep you safe while gardening. Whether you are moving soil around your space, planting seeds, or chopping thick vines, there is a tool or piece of equipment that can help you safely get the job done with less manual effort. Also, all the tools may not be relevant for your space. For instance, you may not need a wheelbarrow if you are gardening in containers on a balcony. I recommend obtaining what you need for what you plan to grow, because you can easily end up with space that is occupied by many pieces of unused equipment. You'll be surprised to see how just a few quality tools can go a long way and for a long time. Lastly, if you are just starting out, the options may be vast and overwhelming, so see the following pages for a list of the most useful tools.

13 USEFUL TOOLS FOR MAINTAINING YOUR GARDEN

TOOL	FUNCTION

Garden boots

Garden boots are designed to keep your feet warm while also protecting them from liquids, dirt, and sharp objects.

Garden hoe

Garden hoes, with their sharp edges, are used to chop through growth and cultivate the soil.

Garden loppers

Garden loppers allow you to access hard-to-reach places to cut through tough, thick, woody branches and stems.

Gloves

Gardening requires much manual labor, and gloves protect the hands from cuts and scrapes that could lead to infection.

Hand cultivator

Hand cultivators are useful for tilling up weeds and aerating areas for planting.

Pruning shears

A sturdy pair of pruning shears is useful for trimming small plants and cutting thick stems and smaller branches.

Rake

Rakes are multifunctional in that they may be used to clear leaves, spread compost, and level soil.

Shovel

Garden shovels are frequently used to dig holes and transport larger amounts of soil from one location to another.

Trowel

Trowels are great for turning and digging out soil for transferring into smaller pots.

Watering can

Watering cans are portable containers that typically carry up to 3 gallons of water. They come in handy when you need to gently hand water your plants.

Watering hose

A watering hose functions by directing water from a larger or continuous source to another location. Sprayer nozzles are typically added to control the flow.

Weed eater

Weed eaters, also known as string trimmers, are used to maintain garden spaces by cutting weeds and trimming small grass.

Wheelbarrow

Wheelbarrows are essential for moving large piles of soil, compost, leaves, and rocks with less effort.

Planning and organizing your ideas will help you create the garden you are imagining.

VISION

The final aspect that should be considered is actually my favorite. It is the vision that you have for your future or present garden, and yourself. Envisioning what you desire your space to look like may provide you with direction and a glimpse into what you hope to accomplish with your garden. You will also be better able to mentally prioritize what you value in your space before it even materializes. Even more, it's important to visualize yourself as the gardener you hope to be, as this will help you focus on what you can expect along the way and how you can best prepare for starting.

To put this into practice, before I start seeds each season I like to visualize what I want the garden to look like, but I don't stop there. I imagine all of the animals and insects that I hope to see and nature sounds that I hope to hear, all signifying that I am cultivating an environment that feels safe and welcoming. I also use that time to imagine how I may work in the garden, and where I could see myself planting seeds and harvesting foods. This action may sound a bit odd, but envisioning costs nothing but time, yet plays a major role in building the confidence you need to begin your gardening journey.

Performing garden tasks like trellising plants can be considered tedious, but such simple acts help the mind slow down and focus on the present moment.

FINDING YOUR "WHY"

Each gardener has different reasons for why they choose to start an edible garden. Some like to garden as a hobby and as an outlet from day-to-day stressors, while others enjoy the practice of cultivating different types of edible plants for wellness. Whatever the reason may be, this forms the foundation of your "why." Of course, some may not think as deeply about why they should start a garden, but this question is a crucial one to ask yourself before beginning because it serves as a guiding light. Understanding why you want or should grow a garden further incentivizes you to not just begin, but also to stick with it. Your purpose will keep you motivated and encouraged, especially when the going gets tough—and trust me, there will be some trying moments along the way and we will cover that soon enough. Yet, despite my emphasizing the need for finding your purpose for gardening, I want to assure you that it's just fine if you don't have a profound reason for why you want to start. When

starting your garden, it is also not necessary to have your rationale completely figured out—that is what the adventure is for and you may even find that your "why" evolves with time. Therefore, a simple curiosity to see whether you are capable of maintaining a garden is also good enough. Whatever sparks that motivation in you, I encourage you to explore and embrace it.

Why is this spark significant? Consider my story. As you read in the previous chapter, I was highly motivated to grow my own food due to the lack of access to better options. Given, I could drive twenty minutes to the grocery store to purchase food, but there is nothing like having direct access to many of the foods my body needs. I previously experienced food insecurity firsthand and I didn't want to experience that again. I wanted to make fresh, diverse, and affordable produce even more accessible to myself and my family. Along with good food options, it was a deep desire of mine to foster a healthy and safe

Growing nutritious food gives me the ability to nutritionally and physically thrive, and this goal has been the driver behind my garden.

environment for the other organisms within my local ecosystem. These desires ultimately turned into my "why" for gardening and growing my own food. Thus, as I prepared to start my first season of gardening, I was so excited to grow dozens of edible plants in my garden beds, and before putting down seeds I spent days imagining what the space could be and why cultivating a harmonious food garden was important to me. This very action is what continuously fed the fire in me to learn whatever I needed to take care of the plants and the life in and around that space. So you see, my "why" was my guiding light.

On a related note, understanding your purpose for gardening may keep you encouraged to press on when challenges arise. For instance, have you ever wanted to accomplish something so badly

that no matter what was thrown at you, something inside of you wouldn't let you give up? I am sure you have. Well, I can't count how many times I have felt frustration, disgust, confusion, and disappointment while gardening, especially when things didn't go as expected or unfortunate mishaps occurred. But all of these emotions are part of the process, and it's what makes the adventure dynamic and rich with lessons. And despite all of the challenges, there was an intrinsic motivation that kept me going—the "why."

It is my objective to help you understand the value of your "why" for cultivating a garden, and how it will push you when you are feeling similar emotions. This, in turn, will help you become not just any type of gardener, but a rather resilient one at that.

ALLOWING YOUR ENVIRONMENT TO MOTIVATE YOU

As you begin to think about how to build your garden, two of the first actionable steps I encourage you to make are (1) taking some time to observe what is around you and (2) identifying the strengths of your environment. I know that these steps may sound a bit vague, so I will explain why this matters.

In order to complement your surroundings, it's a good idea to research some of the elements involved in making the area what it is. Factors such as the local climate, the composition of the soil, and even the types of animals you encounter all make up a local environment. Many of these factors may also be considered strengths, or what contributes to the area's ability to flourish. For instance, if your local climate is somewhere between continental and humid subtropical (meaning you experience hot and humid summers and mild to cold winters), a strength may be that you are able to grow greater plant varieties that are warm-tolerant and cold-tolerant. This may be seen as an advantage because edible plants like corn, tomatoes, and squash thrive in warmer climates,

while plants like collards, broccoli, and leeks thrive in colder climates. So you can say that you get to experience the best of both worlds.

Furthermore, you may find that the composition of your area's soil consists of nutrient-rich sandy loam that requires minimal effort to prepare and amend. That finding alone would be amazing for any gardener, as good soil is the foundation for a good garden. But this information is helpful because it informs you of the health of the ecosystem, above and below ground. Therefore, if the health of the soil is optimal, there is less work you need to do to build up your garden.

Finally, the types of animals that populate your local environment can actually highlight the micro and macro level of biodiversity within the surrounding ecosystem. This is especially important to understand as the plants you may wish to cultivate may be interacting with some or all of these organisms in some way or form. Hence, whatever you observe in the spaces around you can help you understand the type of garden that is best for you and for where you are.

While gardening, it's best to strive for harmony, not perfection. Perfection focuses on you, but harmony focuses on you and your relationship with everything around you.

Next page: The goal of my garden has always been to create an edible landscape that works in harmony with nature.

While evaluating your environment, you may also find that there are noticeable geographical and man-made features present, like dense forestry and rolling hills, or perhaps high-rise buildings with minimal trees. Also, I am sure there are other specific characteristics that drew you to that area as well. Whatever exists around you are the very elements that make your space unique.

To give you a practical example of how this is done, I will explain how I took note of my surroundings prior to constructing my garden. As I detailed in chapter 1, I studied our property for months before drafting even a blueprint for a garden. I suppose you can say that I spent that time connecting with and getting to know the area. I wanted to understand the minute details of what lived there before I came in with new structures and plants—you know, out of respect. During that time, I was able to observe a few things, like how the sun rose and fell over the space, the various species of trees that towered above the yard, the types of birds that often dashed through the space, and the sounds that filled the air as the seasons changed. Of course, there were many more things that I took note of, but each of these provided inspiration for how Tyler and I designed and built our garden.

Now, it may be helpful to elaborate on the significance of these elements, starting with the movement of the sun. This aspect was key because most plants in an edible garden need varying degrees of but consistent sunlight in order to photosynthesize, or convert light into carbohydrates (plant fuel), and the amount of light that is available may determine whether a plant thrives or not. Complementary to the movement of the sun is the presence of trees. Our property consists of several large established trees, such as white oak (*Quercus alba*) and white ash (*Fraxinus americana*). By the way, if you know anything about these trees, you can expect them to reach up to 80 feet (24.4 m) in height when fully grown. Consequently, though these trees are mesmerizing and exude an essence of regality, their height can also block significant light. So, watching the sun's rise and fall throughout the year, while considering the nature of the trees, allowed me to identify the ideal spot for introducing a garden.

Next, I had to be mindful of the other inhabitants of the property, more specifically, the birds. You don't have to be a fan of birds to find the way they look or how they behave fascinating. I was not very curious about birds until I began observing them in my yard. Some of the common bird species here in North Carolina are cardinals, swallows, warblers, and hummingbirds, and all of them exist harmoniously on the property. Recognizing what they eat and where they find shelter meant that I needed to make sure I did not negatively disrupt their way of life by impacting their food source or eliminating their home.

The last element, which may be a bit ambiguous, is the sounds that I often heard as the seasons progressed. Have you ever stood quietly in an environment and just listened to the sounds? Perhaps it sounds like crickets chirping and cicadas buzzing, or maybe not of nature at all, with distant ambulances wailing and cars driving along the street. Since I live in a smaller suburban town, I hear a blend of all of the above sounds, and I focused on creating a space that was accepting of all of it. I realized the mix of all of these species learning to live together is what made my environment unique. So, no matter what sounds you hear, you are able to determine what organisms exist around you and what fits well with respect to that space. Quite frankly, this provides immense inspiration and motivation for the types of gardens you may consider.

In summary, observing and taking notes from the environment around you can teach you much about what you need in order to grow the garden you desire in a harmonious manner. As I continue to garden each year, I am realizing that sometimes there is no need to revise what nature has already mastered. Give honor to what is already in your environment, welcome the inspiration, and then use that as a launchpad to motivate yourself to build the garden that is best for you.

Japanese beetles are undoubtedly a pain in the United States, but with consistent pest management and monitoring you can mitigate the risk of damage to your garden.

THERE WILL BE VALLEYS AND TRIALS

Unfortunately, I have to slightly pivot from the inspiration into what some may call the tribulation. As much as I would love to only lay out all of the beauty and success that you may experience, it wouldn't be realistic or fair to you if I neglected to emphasize the potential adversity you may face. But don't worry, as I highlight a few examples of trials that may be experienced while gardening, I will also detail how they may be overcome.

There will be moments where you may want to give up and quit, and here is where knowing your "why" also becomes a motivating factor. Gardening requires us to extend and challenge ourselves in ways that we may not every day. Yet, in those moments, I hear the voice of my grandfather say, "When the going gets tough, you gotta just keep on keepin' on." That is strong wisdom, but what does it look like in practice?

In the image on page 78 are carrots that were pulled from the bed in my first year of gardening. I waited for nearly three months to pull these carrots, and to my dismay this was the product. I will admit, I had a mix of emotions ranging from disappointment to confusion, as I could not understand what I did wrong. However, after lifting my head and adjusting my sad face, I researched what the issue could

There are many reasons (such as nutritional deficiency, suboptimal temperatures, compacted soil, and pathogens) that may explain why carrots grow stunted or underdeveloped. Once you find the source of your issue, you are well on your way to growing healthy carrots.

Each year we plant cucumbers knowing that we are not the only ones who find the fruits delicious. Pictured here is evidence of destruction by a common southeast pest known as the pickleworm (*Diaphania nitidalis*).

be and the result was compacted soil. Compacted soil can cause a number of issues for root vegetables like carrots mainly because it serves as a barrier for the downward growth that takes place. Due to this impeded growth, you may see skinny, hairy, deformed, or underdeveloped carrots. Fortunately there is a solution for this, and I was able to remedy this issue for the next season by doing three things: tilling up the soil and removing rocks and hard balls of clay, adding a bit more compost and balanced fertilizer to replace the lost nutrients, and adding perlite (an amorphous volcanic glass used to help loosen soil). Employing each of these solutions helped the carrots grow optimally in the following season.

Secondly, there are the pickleworm moths, which, in the larval stage of their development, cause the most destruction to cucurbit fruits. Thinking about this pest takes me back to growing pickling cucumbers in my second year. I kid you not, I was ready to pull up everything and commit to never growing another cucumber. Pickleworms, with their aggressive eating habits, have the ability to traumatize you by creeping their way into your fruits as they destroy your crop. What makes this somewhat gross is that you may not realize they have infested your fruits until you open or slice them. This is also why I examine all produce, especially the cucurbits. Thankfully, you won't be walking completely into the dark growing these, as there is a telltale sign that a pickleworm has made its way in—small circular holes appear on the outside surface with soft fruit frass. After much gagging, and ultimately deciding not to give up, I searched for a solution. Interestingly, the female moth that lays these eggs is nocturnal, so a solution was simply covering the cucumber plants at night with a lightweight row cover. The next round of cucumbers planted that season were able to flourish.

The last example that I will detail is of the larger animals that find joy in consuming fresh garden goods, just like us humans. In the case of my garden and many others, it is the rabbits and deer. As sweet and precious as these animals may appear, they can be brazen when it comes to eating your garden produce, especially the items they enjoy most, like fruits and leafy greens. I recall one season growing corn and cabbage in two of our lowest garden beds. Mind you, at the time the garden did not have any physical barriers or delineations from the forest, so the space was open and welcoming to everyone and everything. At this moment, you may be thinking, "Wow, you were setting yourself up for garden decimation." And in hindsight I would agree, but I had never seen either a rabbit or a deer on our property until we began gardening. Furthermore, there is a saying that goes, "If something is not eating your plants, then your garden is not part of the ecosystem." Needless to say, the deer and rabbits devoured my corn and cabbage plants. Of course I was upset, because I had waited so long for these vegetables to reach maturity for harvesting, but clearly so did the animals. This situation was rectified by constructing a wire fence and growing companion plants and highly aromatic herbs around the garden perimeter. Since I implemented this strategy, the deer and rabbits find food outside of the garden, and we are able to coexist without destruction to the garden or their living space.

Rabbits, like people, tend to enjoy many of the foods in the garden, but you can repel them by putting up fencing or netting.

The takeaway here is that the trials make you a stronger gardener and encourage you to learn more about how the environment and plants around you function. But knowing the purpose, or my "why" for growing nutritious food for me and my family, is the very thing that kept me going. By highlighting my challenges, I hope that you can avoid them, but if you are unable to, may you stay motivated to keep on keepin' on.

DIRT IS NOT YOUR ENEMY

When I was a child, I enjoyed playing outside with my younger brother each day after school. My parents never had a problem with our outdoor activities, but I vividly remember my mom telling us quite frequently, "You guys, please try not to get so dirty today. You don't want germs, do you?" Of course, memories of the aftermath elude me, but I am sure that I gave an honest effort to stay clean and tidy.

From then on I tried to avoid getting dirty—that is, until I started gardening. Sorry, Mom! And to answer your question, actually yes, I do want the germs, but I'll tell you why. In general, getting soiled by stuff on the ground has generally been discouraged. Whether you grew up in a household where cleanliness was encouraged or sought to avoid messing up your clothes as an adult, the idea of getting dirty is universally not praised. However, an interesting study done by a group at the University of Colorado showed the benefits of microbes in soil and the possible beneficial effects they may have on our health. The research specifically highlighted *Mycobacterium vaccae*, a bacterium commonly found in soil that stimulates brain cells to produce the chemical serotonin. Though this study was performed in mice, there are several other qualitative and quantitative studies that have taken place over the years that further substantiate the positive impact that soil may have on human health. What this may suggest is that some of the germs in soil may in fact be good for us. Did you hear that, Mom? Now wait, before I get carried away into germ land, the responsible thing to do is acknowledge that there are some very real pathogens (or bad germs) that can cause serious negative effects on our health, and some of these organisms exist within the soil, so it is important that you wear gloves and avoid getting soil in your eyes and mouth.

Embrace and connect with the soil that you plan to grow your garden in; it fosters respect for every organism's role in the process.

Before I proceed with the benefits, I want to clarify two terms that are often used interchangeably, "soil" and "dirt." Oftentimes people refer to the two terms synonymously, but if you asked a gardener or anyone who studies soil chemistry and health, I'm sure they will beg to differ. Macroscopically and at a quick glance, dirt and soil may appear the same, but if you look closer, perhaps under a microscope, you will see that their compositions are distinct. Dirt comprises clay, sand, and rocks and typically lacks structure and texture. Most importantly, the major characteristic of dirt is that it does not support life. On the contrary, soil consists of organic matter, living organisms, and essential minerals and nutrients necessary for growing and sustaining life. In summary, one substance is considered dead, and one substance is considered living. So, by now you may be wondering, how then is dirt not my enemy? And my response to that is simple: Although dirt is dead, it can be amended and revitalized to become a medium that is conducive to growth. This is typically done with soil amendments like fertilizers and compost, which is broken-down organic matter (like animal products and plant and food scraps) that can be added to improve soil. But like anything worth working for, compost requires a bit of sweat, muscle, and tenacity.

Let's continue with these health benefits, shall we? After a long day, have you ever walked out into nature, whether at a park, in the mountains, or even in your own yard, and as soon as you engaged with the elements, you experienced a wave of peace or perhaps bliss? Even if you don't consider yourself a nature person it's not by happenstance that immersing yourself in nature can evoke these feelings. Spending time in the garden may lead to a similar experience. The very act of handling soil allows you to examine its condition and prepare it for growing plants while engaging with an entire ecosystem filled with living organisms that may benefit your well-being, like the *Mycobacterium vaccae*. As I stated above, maintaining the vibrance of soil is one the most crucial steps in gardening, as it is the foundation for life in the garden. For this reason, there is much work that goes into amending, feeding, and fortifying a healthy soil base, even if you are working with dirt.

In the process of learning to garden, I had a lot to learn about everything—plants, soil, climate, and much more. Even though I have a scientific background, sometimes nature surprised me with unpredictable curveballs. I struggled with this

Cured, nutrient-dense compost is the foundation of rich and healthy soil, especially in edible gardens.

because the curveballs typically resulted in a disappointing outcome. In the first year of our garden, our city was hit by a tornado, and the violent winds knocked down a few of our vegetable plants and all ten of our tomato plants. At the time, I was devastated, as I felt that all our planning and hard work on those tomato plants were a waste. As I tell this story now, I can't help but chuckle, because looking back I know going through and overcoming those types of challenges are necessary. Needless to say, Tyler and I put in additional time and sweat to fix the damages in the garden and worked on stabilizing the tomato plants. In turn, that ended up being our best tomato season. The lesson is that plants are resilient, and so are we.

In addition to the curveballs, gardening often presents some scary and even disgusting experiences. Remember back in chapter 1 when I hinted that I had a story about frogs? Well, this is a great time for another moment of transparency. Are you ready? Okay. I have a phobia of frogs and toads. I mean this phobia was the real deal from childhood until adulthood. There are so many types of frogs and toads, and many range from small to large, from moist and smooth to dry and bumpy. No matter the size, shape, or species, all of them stir anxiety within me. So, there, you now know my secret. I am also aware that I talked about their impact on the environment a while back with such zeal and confidence that my sentiments almost seem contradictory. However, I bring this vulnerable element to you to say that scary stuff happens, but you will learn that even the scary stuff has its purpose.

Although I would like to avoid close encounters with frogs and toads, I value them in this world and in my growing space—they are needed for the balance of the ecosystem. Over the years, I began to see fewer frogs, and though I was relieved, I was curious as to what prompted the decline. And while

Maintaining a compost pile facilitates the breakdown of organic matter into nutrient-rich fertilizer that is later used to improve soil structure and composition.

there are many reasons for this phenomenon, like pollution of their habitats, displacement, and new predators, I have learned to look to the frogs for ecological changes. The presence of frogs in the garden is perhaps a sign of equilibrium within the ecosystem, and a gift that I had to learn to accept and appreciate.

As you garden, you may find yourself facing legitimate fears head-on, and honestly, at times it may be downright dirty, disgusting, and terrifying. Your heart may skip a beat, you may spontaneously tear up, shriek, and perhaps run, but as you become a gardener you will learn to accept and embrace that there will be dirty moments and you will get dirty. The dirt is not your enemy, and it never will be. Disappointments and fearful occurrences are inevitable, but in all of those is an opportunity to cultivate rich soil out of dirt, which lays the foundation for growth.

Opposite: There will be times where extensive labor may be required to overcome the challenges, but that is how resilience is built.

ENCOURAGEMENT CORNER

COMMON CHALLENGES FOR BEGINNING GARDENERS

Gardening is a never-ending learning process, so believe it or not, many pitfalls are common to both beginner and veteran gardeners. First, like people, all plants need food to thrive, but not all food is good for all plants. Mishaps with fertilizers are a big problem starting out. The quality and quantity of fertilizer that you use can either promote or hinder growth. Sometimes, adding the wrong type or adding too much will not only harm your plants but may also potentially leave unfavorable residuals in your garden bed. To avoid this, it is best to research the types of nutrients each of your plants needs, the best fertilizers with minimal long-term effects, and how frequently you should feed your plants.

Secondly, trying to grow certain plants out of their recommended season is a challenge for many. Growing plants in the right season ensures that they are growing in their preferred element for optimal production. Sometimes it is more obvious which plants should be grown in each season, but other times it is not. Most seed packets and plants

Regular feedings with a quality plant-specific fertilizer keep the microorganisms within your soil and the plants in your garden flourishing.

come with a guide for the best growing dates. Additionally, you can check out your local agricultural extension center's website for growing specific things in your area.

Lastly, being unaware of your geographic area's range of climatic conditions or hardiness zone may pose a pitfall and will easily make anyone feel as if they do not possess a green thumb, when in actuality a green thumb is nurtured, not inherited. Ecoregion maps take into account your area's precipitation habits, soil composition, and biodiversity characteristics. Understanding details around both your hardiness zone and your ecoregion sets you up for success and helps you identify what can be grown in your area. I have had my fair share of trying to grow a few things like oranges and other tropical fruits in North Carolina (where the lowest average temperature range is between 5°F and 10°F

[-15°C and -12.2°C]) that were ideally grown in southeast Florida (where the lowest average temperature range is between 35°F and 40°F [1.7°C and 4.4°C]), and these experiments did not work out well. As a matter of fact, most did not grow and for the ones that did grow, they did not reach maturity before the first frost date. I am since over that disappointment, and I can laugh at it now. If you reside in the United States, a great resource to identify your hardiness zone is the U.S. Department of Agriculture's website. This resource will tell you all you need to know and more.

There will be times when you get frustrated (especially with pests, diseases, and animals), but it helps to learn how to work with nature and not against it. Challenges and failures make for fertile ground to plant seeds of success. Things will happen beyond your control, but once you can accept and learn from it, you will be able to grow beyond it. This is the journey to becoming a gardener.

The *Trichoplusia ni*, or cabbage looper larvae, can destroy cruciferous vegetables, like this kale, overnight. Diligent pest control can help you successfully grow these vegetables.

PERSPECTIVES OF A GARDENER

Meet Resh Gala
Location: New Jersey
Social Media Handles: @reshgala and
@hundredtomatoes
Website: reshgala.com

MY GARDENING JOURNEY

I am a self-taught gardener and have been gardening for the last five years. Over the years, I have learned many lessons from my failures and experiences in the garden, but it was during the most recent public health crisis that resulted in lockdowns, food scarcity, and rationing in the grocery stores that I realized I wanted to become as self-sufficient as possible and not depend on others for access to food.

Resh standing next to an overflow of fresh fruits and vegetables straight out of her New Jersey home garden.

Having experienced firsthand the benefits of gardening, for my physical and mental well-being, I wanted to make a positive impact on my community and the planet too. I founded my company, Hundred Tomatoes, which designs, consults on, and installs edible, organic gardens in New Jersey and surrounding areas, and our mission is to encourage people to grow their own food and live their best lives. There is no right or wrong way to garden—it's simply about getting started.

MOTIVATION TO BEGIN

When I began my gardening journey, I honestly did not have any expectations—just a sense of curiosity and fun. My first time was a huge failure because I was a novice and didn't know much about effectively maintaining a garden. At that time, I purchased two tomato plants from a big-box retailer and ended up harvesting only two small tomatoes with a disease called blossom-end rot. Of course, I was so disappointed, but that did not stop me from trying to grow food. On my second try, I hired a landscaper to build small raised beds for me, but they ended up being filled with poor-quality topsoil. So, you can imagine that again nothing grew and my plants were ridden with pests and disease. This led me down the path of reading about and researching more organic and environmentally friendly gardening practices. Through my research, I found that there was one repetitive theme everywhere—

good soil is the foundation of a good garden. Now it is my goal to always foster a healthy soil environment while growing my food.

EDIBLE GARDENING AND FOOD SOVEREIGNTY

Gardening has given me a great sense of accomplishment, empowerment, and positivity. The act of taking a small seed or plant, nurturing it, and helping it to thrive makes me believe that I have created something of value in this world. I also believe that this is the case with food. Food is valuable, and if you have the ability to grow it, you also have the ability to achieve food sovereignty!

HOW GARDENING INFLUENCES MY PERSPECTIVE ON FOOD AND THE ENVIRONMENT

Gardening has definitely made me more aware of how much food waste we produce as human beings. As consumers, sometimes when we visit grocery stores, we get to see how much food is available to us, and we are often unaware of where and how these foods are produced. In these instances, I have found that it's easy to purchase more than we need, and this abundance frequently goes to waste. However, when growing our own food, we tend to become more mindful of the time and effort (from nature and ourselves) that goes into growing each food item, and we value it more—so much so that we don't want to see any part wasted. I understand firsthand the time and effort it takes to grow my food. Now, I'm more inclined to eat vegetables that are imperfect or not my favorite, and have found ways to preserve them for later consumption. Food is to be appreciated, not wasted, and gardening has helped me further appreciate every factor that contributes to the food that I need for survival.

EMPOWERED TO GROW NEW FOODS

I absolutely love experimenting in the garden. Gardening has empowered me to not just grow what I like to eat, but also try new things that I've never tried before! Recently, I took a few store-bought potatoes that had sprouted in my pantry, buried them in the garden, and turned them into an incredible harvest ninety days later! I can happily say that I've grown strawberries from tiny seeds, moringa and stevia plants, and found a new favorite fruit: Aunt Molly's ground cherry! My family and friends know that I'm always searching for new varieties of vegetables to grow each year, especially the most flavorful tomatoes. I highly recommend you try 'Aunt Ruby's German Green' tomato!

Resh's meticulously organized garden overflowing with large, lush leafy greens and peppers.

CHAPTER 4

SOWING GOOD SEEDS

Evaluating Seed Options for Your Garden

In the previous chapter, I spoke about the role that soil plays in the production of edible plants, but there is another component that is fundamental to most plants, and that is the seed. As you may know, seeds form as a result of an ovule being fertilized through pollination. Therefore, a seed is the embryonic stage of a plant that is typically enclosed in some protective outside covering. While some protective coverings are hard, others may be softer; either way, the coverings help the internal embryo and nutritive tissue, called the endosperm, maintain viability. Seeds vary in size, texture, and weight and their morphology is completely based upon the genetics of the parent plant. Okay, I had to give that brief biology lesson so that we can walk with greater understanding into the importance of seeds in gardening.

Opposite: These seeds are so tiny, yet they hold a wonderfully divine purpose—becoming food that gives us sustenance.

SEED FUNDAMENTALS

The type of seed you begin with can either make or break your garden plans, especially if you've invested a significant amount of funds in procuring them. There have been many people who assumed they were not good growers of plants because either they could not get their seeds to germinate or the plants did not turn out the way they expected. So, though I encourage you to explore your own gardening journey, I also hope to set you up for success, and a major part of that success will lie in your seeds. When evaluating seed options to plant in your garden, there are a few factors that may be helpful to consider, such as the age of the seeds, how the seeds were produced, and whether chemicals were used in their growing process. These are crucial factors because each will help you understand the quality of the seeds you hope to use and what you can expect as they mature.

A major part of planning for your garden is getting your supplies cleaned and organized for planting seeds.

In order to grow vigorous and prolific plants, the types of seeds you select must be of good quality.

SEED AGE

When searching for seeds, many gardeners first check out the date by which the seeds should be used. If your seeds are commercially produced, this date is typically found somewhere on the seed packet; if they are not, the grower should know when the seeds were harvested and by what date they are best used. The age of seeds is particularly important because, over time, if seeds are not prepared for long-term storage, they gradually lose their viability, or ability to germinate and produce. Therefore, for the best outcome it is best to begin your plants with fresh seeds that are under two years old. This isn't to say that seeds older than two years will not do well, as I have experienced a few selections that have defied the statistics but this was most likely due to the nature of the plant. Some seeds, like onion, spinach, and parsley, simply have a shorter shelf life than seeds like artichokes, tomatoes, and melons. Yet statistically speaking, after two years of age the germination rate of many seeds begins to decline. Consequently, when you are searching for seeds to get your garden started, I recommend procuring those that are the freshest and newest in age.

A variety of squash and eggplants grown using heirloom seeds, so their seeds will be saved and used for future seasons.

OPEN-POLLINATED SEEDS AND HYBRID SEEDS

Now that I have covered the value in selecting fresh seeds, I will explain how pollination methods may affect the seeds that are produced. If you recall the brief biology lesson on how seeds are formed, there is a necessary step that is required, and that is pollination, or the transferring of pollen from the male part to the ovule, the female part. The process is not just important for the formation of seeds, but more specifically, for the passing down of genes. Which brings us to how this is relevant to the quality of seeds. There are a few ways in which the pollination of plants can occur, but I will highlight two: open pollination and hybridization.

Open pollination is quite simple in that it occurs by natural mechanisms, meaning by way of birds, insects, and wind. Through this method, the plants produced are generally more genetically diverse and adapted to the local environment. More importantly, plants produced through open pollination grow true-to-type, or the same as the parent plant.

Through open pollination, heirloom or generational plants may be produced and continually passed down. You will also find that these heirloom varieties are highly desired by gardeners who enjoy regrowing plants from seeds saved during the season.

In contrast, hybridization is a more controlled method of pollinating plants and you will typically see different species or varieties being crossed through human intervention. Because of this control in plant breeding, the hybridization method is preferred by many commercial producers. While you can choose a desired trait for a plant through this method, it's important to remember that these seeds can't be saved due to their genetic instability. So therein lies the dilemma: You may get a one-of-a-kind plant, but it may unfortunately be less vigorous than those produced through open pollination, and you will most likely have to continue purchasing the seeds the following seasons. Whether you have access to heirloom or hybrid seeds, growing a wide variety of plants is possible—it just depends which one you prefer, and perhaps you opt for trying both.

ORGANIC AND NONORGANIC SEEDS

You may hear the terms "organic" and "nonorganic" when it comes to seeds, but what differentiates the two and how do you choose? Over the years, and as gardening has become more popular, many commercial suppliers and big-box stores have made significant efforts to offer both organic and non-organic seed options. Often they are marketed side by side, so if you are not reading the packet, it's easy to overlook which one you have. The differences between organic and nonorganic seeds lie in how the parent plants were cultivated. Organic seeds derive from plants that have not encountered treatments with synthetic chemicals, fertilizers, or pesticides at any point in their development. These organically produced plants are grown using simple methods that seek to emulate and support the surrounding ecosystem. There are thousands of varieties of organic seeds available, from vegetables and fruits to flowers and herbs, and recently they have become more accessible. Some countries have federal guidelines that a grower, especially one who intends to sell plants and seeds, must adhere to in order to be certified as an organic gardener or farmer. This classification is given after a rigorous inspection process.

Conversely, nonorganic seeds are produced through parent plants that have encountered synthetic chemicals, fertilizers, or pesticides. This nonorganic classification is rather unique in that even if the plant has not directly encountered synthetic chemicals with the intention of greater growth advantage, it can still be affected by residual chemicals in the soil or in the groundwater. This is why many growers and agricultural agencies perform tests on the seeds, plants, and soil to analyze their composition and potential exposure to specific substances.

Why are synthetic chemicals used in the first place? Many growers, especially commercial gardeners and farmers, want to maximize production in

Heirloom seeds are often preferred by gardeners because they are able to retain their true traits from generation to generation.

a more efficient way. Though there is scientific data that suggests that the use of synthetic chemicals may have negative effects on the ecosystem, there are many reasons why they have been used: to mitigate crop destruction due to pathogens and pests, to maximize crops by eliminating weeds, and to increase yields. Luckily, more ecologically conscious chemical formulations are becoming more prevalent and accessible to growers of all experience levels.

Finally, I leave you with this: the quality of your seeds can greatly determine the success of your garden, and making sure you purchase seeds from reliable suppliers will be key. Furthermore, knowing how fresh your seeds are and how they were produced will let you know whether you are sowing good seeds in the earth. Still, you have options and the autonomy to choose what works best for you where you are. The most important thing is that you sow good seeds in your garden, and within yourself.

NURTURING YOUR SEEDS

So you now have your seeds and are ready to get growing, but how do ensure that you are providing your seeds with the best shot at success? There are times when gardeners obtain high-quality seeds, but due to improper nurturing, the seeds do not perform well. The reason for poor performance may include improper storage, nutrient deficiency, insufficient spacing, or inadequate light, and these factors play a key role in the rate of development and whether the plant produces as intended. Therefore, we will spend some time discussing how to properly nourish your seeds to achieve optimal germination and development, beginning with recommendations on how to store your seeds.

As a gardener, you can easily accumulate many varieties of seeds, as it's exciting to plan for all of the possible plants to grow; trust me—I've been there. Yet, what many may not realize is that proper storage can prolong the shelf life of your seeds, sometimes for several years. The most important thing to keep in mind when storing your seeds is to maintain a cool, dry, and dark location. Warmth, moisture, and light will kick-start the development of your seeds, and that is not what you want when storing them. So, when selecting a storage method, consider locations that will provide the correct environment. Fortunately, this is where many gardeners get creative, using dark paper envelopes, photo album containers, and upcycled jewelry boxes. In my case, I have found using a craft bead storage container allows me to easily transport seeds, and it keeps them organized in an airtight environment. Of course, this is not necessary, and you may keep your seeds in their original packaging if you choose. Regardless of which method you choose, let your imagination run wild while keeping in mind the three crucial factors for proper seed storage.

Seed-starting cups and trays provide plants an optimal environment until they have matured enough to be transplanted into their more permanent beds.

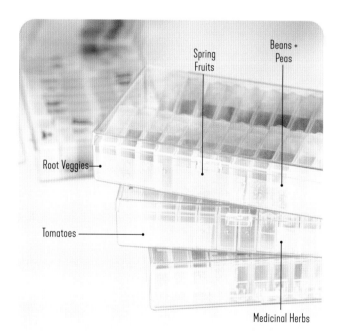

Spring Fruits

Beans + Peas

Root Veggies

Tomatoes

Medicinal Herbs

Seed organization is vital for protecting the quality of your seeds and keeping track of what you have. This container is simply a craft bead organizer that I repurposed.

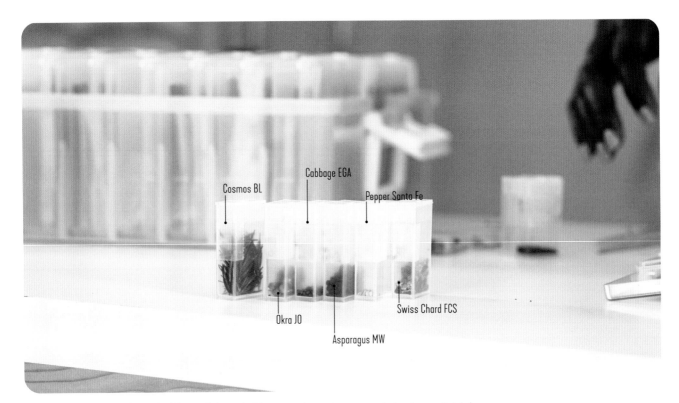

Cosmos BL

Cabbage EGA

Pepper Santa Fe

Okra JO

Asparagus MW

Swiss Chard FCS

Proper seed storage is crucial to seed viability, so it's best to look for storage that can keep your seeds dry, clean, and labeled.

When you purchase seeds for the garden, there are three things I recommend: Ensure that the seeds are from a reliable supplier, that they contain basic growing instructions, and that the seeds are packaged properly. This information will help you know who produced the seeds, best practices for helping them grow, and whether they will do well once you plant them.

Ensuring that your seeds are produced by a reliable supplier is a very important first step, in that you want to make sure your seeds are uncontaminated by harmful substances, that they will grow optimally, and that they will produce the plant that they are labeled as. For instance, I remember an odd phenomenon that recently occurred where many people around the globe were randomly receiving unrequested, unlabeled, unsourced seeds through the mail. Needless to say, local agricultural agencies urged people to destroy them or submit them to the agency. The lesson here is knowing the source of your seeds leaves you better informed of what you are putting into your garden.

Most suppliers include information on their packaging about general growing instructions that may be tailored to your climate and region. These instructions highlight tips such as seed count, ideal planting depth, spacing, lighting, temperatures, when to sow, and days to maturity. Some seed packets may also provide instructions for storing. These little nuggets of advice are fairly easy to follow and time-savers when you are planning out your garden. Lastly, the way in which seeds are packaged by suppliers will determine how well they perform once they get to your garden. I recommend looking for seeds that are in moisture-proof packaging that can provide general protection against normal handling, while maintaining the physical integrity of the seeds within.

Now let's cover what most seeds need to thrive. I'm sure that you have heard of the three fundamental components that seeds need to grow: good

This lemon balm, a perennial herb, was cultivated from seed and has thrived over the course of two years.

lighting, good medium, and sufficient water. Light can either stimulate or inhibit the germination of seeds. Some plants, including impatiens, begonias, lettuce, and kale, require a regular lighting schedule to help them germinate, while other plants, like verbena, calendula, and phlox, prefer to germinate in darkness. Knowing what type of lighting your seeds require will foster optimal germination.

Secondly, the medium in which you grow your seeds, whether it is water or soil, should consist of a structure that gives roots space to spread and the ability for water and nutrients to penetrate. This is what makes hydroponic gardening so interesting, as growing in aqueous solutions does not technically have a defined structure, yet water, nutrients, and airflow are all incorporated, thus allowing plants to thrive.

Thirdly, sufficient water (even in the form of humidity) will initiate the germination process. As I highlighted before, a consistent flow of water is needed to keep nutrients circulating, but even more,

water softens the seed coat, allowing the embryo to make contact with the soil.

Two other factors needed to get your seeds beyond the germination stage are adequate seed spacing and optimal nourishment. Seed spacing refers to the amount of distance you plant one seed from another. This is essential, because depending on your spacing you can increase yields, decrease the chance for disease spread, and minimize having your seeds compete with one another for resources. The methods you use to nurture your seeds will make all the difference in how they develop. Learning how to best care for your seeds will foster the nurturer within you, and understanding how to get your plants from surviving mode to thriving mode will help you appreciate the role that you play as a steward of your garden.

Next page: Finding a designated spot near your garden and reliable supplies help keep you organized and efficient while working with your seeds.

ASHLIE'S DOZEN

TOMATOES

When you're starting your edible garden journey, tomatoes are a great beginner's plant. Whether you choose to purchase transplants or grow your tomatoes from seed, this plant is guaranteed to keep even the best gardeners motivated to grow their own food. As one of my family's favorites, this heat-loving fruit is easy to grow, durable, and a highly prolific producer when given the proper care. An additional advantage to growing tomatoes is the many delicious varieties to select from—sweet and tangy to earthy and mild. Depending on your preferences, there are a myriad of recipes that can be prepared using garden-fresh tomatoes. If tomatoes are started from seeds, the variety selection may reach well into the hundreds. There are many vendors from which plants and seeds can be purchased, so whether you opt for growing your tomatoes from transplants or seeds you are sure to have a plethora of options to choose from.

Tomato Growth

One important factor to consider when growing tomatoes is their growing habits, or whether they are determinate or indeterminate. Determinate cultivars (such as the 'Beefsteak' and 'Roma') are bushier and typically produce their fruits on the ends of their branches. Most determinate tomato plants are compact growers and have a sturdy main stem, in which minimal support is required. Alternatively, indeterminate cultivars (such as 'Brandywine' and 'Cherokee Purple') vine or climb until they are forced to stop growing. Unlike the determinate varieties, the indeterminate tomatoes produce fruits from the sides of the stem, which in turns allows the main stem to focus on continuous growth. Of course, this means that these plants gen-

Vintage wine tomatoes produce a sweet, bright red and striped fruit that complements almost any savory dish, especially pastas.

erally require support and consistent maintenance.

In addition to their growing ease, tomatoes have a fairly long growing season and will provide consistent harvests throughout the spring, summer, and into early fall. As you search through tomato varieties, it is also important to note that most, if not all, are frost-intolerant, so plant transplants after your area's average last frost date and seeds approximately six weeks before your last frost date. This will ensure optimal germination and production.

Tomato Harvests

Harvest time is undoubtedly one of the highlights of growing tomatoes. Color change of the fruit is typically the first indicator of the natural ripening process and helps with determining the ideal time to harvest the fruits. Some gardeners choose to harvest at the first sign of ripening, while others wait until the tomatoes are fully ripe. Whichever your preference, one thing remains true: There is nothing like the taste of a vine-ripened tomato straight off the bush.

ASHLIE'S DOZEN

This single cayenne pepper plant may produce up to seventy peppers in one season.

PEPPERS

Peppers are vegetables that we grow each year here in North Carolina. In addition to their culinary versatility, the harvests are plentiful. Peppers will always be on my list of recommended plants to grow, as there are so many colorful varieties, such as bell, banana, shishito, habanero, and jalapeño. Each variety possesses a distinct flavor profile, ranging from fruity and mild to hot and spicy. Many gardeners opt for picking their peppers while green; however, if you allow the peppers to ripen on the vine, the flavor will be richer and perhaps even sweeter. Peppers taste wonderful in both their ripened and unripened state and have a high nutritional value, loaded with essential vitamins and minerals.

Pepper Growth

Like tomatoes, peppers are easy to grow and share a preference for long, warm growing seasons. However, the germination process is slow. When peppers are grown from seeds, the germination window can range from seven to twenty-one days. To ensure optimal development, seeds should be maintained at a consistent temperature of 82°F to 90°F (27.8°C to 32.2°C). Luckily, peppers are common vegetables grown in gardens, so seedlings and transplants are easily accessible. Procuring seedlings or growing your own seedlings for transplanting may also save time, allowing for an earlier start. I've found that as pepper plants mature, they do not require much maintenance except for consistent watering and a steady fertilizing schedule. Lastly, one great benefit to growing peppers is that most pests (aphids are the exception) steer clear of these plants.

Pepper Harvests

Though I highlighted their slow germination time, once peppers hit their growth stride, you can expect an abundance throughout the season. Besides eating some varieties fresh off the vine, we get creative to enjoy them as stuffed peppers, salsas, and pepper jams.

ASHLIE'S DOZEN

Sweet basil, a commonly grown herb, has a flavor profile that is comparable to both mint and anise.

BASIL

Basil is a popular herb grown by many gardeners all over, and it's obvious why—it is versatile and delicious. This garden favorite is a warm-weather annual herb that grows well in full sun and well-draining, nutrient-rich soil. Additionally, basil grows well with a few other vegetables on this list, like tomatoes, root vegetables, and peppers. When planted alongside these plants, its foliage doubles as ground cover, while its aroma helps repel pests.

Basil Growth

Each spring I look forward to planting various types of basil: 'Sweet Thai', 'Genovese', and 'Dark Opal' are a few of my favorites. Each variety is used for specific dishes. For instance, 'Sweet Thai' basil is used in Asian-inspired dishes like homemade ramen and soups. 'Genovese' basil, with its mouthwatering clove-like flavor, is harvested by the handful and added into my homemade pasta sauces or on top of freshly sliced tomatoes. 'Dark Opal' basil, with its sweet and earthy flavor, is typically dehydrated and used as seasonings or in herbal teas.

I recommend growing this herb between temperatures of 70°F and 80°F (21°C and 26.7°C), as I have found this range to be the sweet spot. When growing conditions are consistently ideal, you can expect the plants to reach a height between 12 inches (30.5 cm) and even 36 inches (91 cm). But be especially careful of growing this herb in cooler temperatures, as it is frost-intolerant. The good news is, this plant is not limited to just growing outdoors, as it also does well in indoor gardens. We typically plant these in our vertical garden beds so that the sweet herbal aroma welcomes us as soon as we walk into the garden.

Basil Harvests

The taste of basil is so delectable that I often find myself snipping and wrapping pieces of leaves around other vegetables that I have picked as I walk through the garden. This plant is a favorite not only for me, but also for the pollinators. If you allow a few plants to flower, the bees will buzz with gratitude.

KALE

Kale is a fast-growing leafy green that is a staple in our garden. Why? Because it only takes about two months to mature from seed, and it can be used for many dishes. Known for its inability to wilt, this green offers much versatility in recipes, such as salads and vegetable wraps. Depending on the variety and when it is cultivated, kale is fantastic steamed with a dash of sea salt or blended in a fresh fruit and green smoothie. A few of my favorite varieties are 'Red Russian', 'Purple Moon', 'Dwarf Green Curled Vates', and 'Nero di Toscana'. Many people feel that kale's flavor profile is fairly unremarkable; however, I disagree, and you may as well. The 'Red Russian' and 'Purple Moon' varieties feature purple-veining foliage and have a crisp yet sweet flavor. These are perfect as colorful salad greens. The 'Dwarf Green Curled Vates', with its tightly curled, bluish-green leaves, is cold-weather hardy and sweet when freshly cut. It also adds great nutrients and texture to a warm stew or soup. The 'Nero di Toscana' variety (commonly known as dinosaur kale), with its dark, puckered leaves, is delicious lightly sautéed in olive oil with garlic. You will thank me once you try it.

Curly kale is a fast-growing leafy green that is easy to cultivate. In our household, we eat kale frequently, so we grow seven varieties in our garden.

Kale Growth

Though we are able to grow kale throughout the year, it produces the best flavor in cooler temperatures or after a good frost. We typically start these seeds indoors in a well-draining potting soil/compost mix and transplant them out eight weeks before the first frost or right at the beginning of spring. Once transplanted, space them out about 18 inches (45.7 cm) apart, as they can grow up to 24 inches (61 cm) in height, depending on the variety and growing conditions. Kale plants grow best in full sun but can tolerate partial shade.

Kale Harvests

Kale harvests are plentiful. The leaves can be picked in the baby leaf stage for fresh eating in salads. Or it can be harvested as mature leaves that are best for cooking.

ASHLIE'S DOZEN

SWISS CHARD

If I had to describe the taste of Swiss chard I would say it is a mix between beets and spinach, and technically I would be spot-on because chard is in the same family as beets and is also known as leaf beet or spinach beet. Swiss chard, or simply chard, is mostly grown for its leafy tops, but its root is edible. However, because most of the energy of the plant goes to developing the leaves, the root is hard and fibrous, so it may not be as palatable as a beet. I enjoy using this nutrient-dense green the same way I would prepare spinach: in salads and sandwiches.

We started this white chard plant in early spring, and in a matter of two months it has provided us with a delicious harvest of crisp, sweet leaves. Butternut squash and chard soup is a favorite around here.

Chard Growth

There are many varieties of chard, but a few of the major ones are 'Rhubarb Red', 'Fordhook Giant', 'Magenta Sunset', and 'Orange Fantasia'. We typically go for the 'Bright Lights' variety, which produces colorful crunchy stems and large, glossy, crinkled leaves. And by colorful, I mean gold, red, orange, pink, purple, and white. Not only does this plant add pops of vibrant color in the garden, but it's also an easygoing, low-maintenance plant to cultivate. Like many plants on this list, chard grows well in loose, well-draining, neutral-pH soil. You can easily grow this plant from spring through fall and even into the winter if you live in warmer climates. Here in North Carolina, chard plants have fared well through the peak of winter. One interesting characteristic to remember about this green is that it is a biennial plant, which means that it has a life cycle of two years. Therefore, this plant can be harvested in the first year and second year before it flowers and produces seeds. I highly recommend growing this plant, as it looks lovely in the garden and is delectable on the plate.

Chard Harvests

Like kale, chard can be harvested as a baby green or as a mature leaf. The baby greens are delicious in salad blends while the fully grown leaves are best cooked. Their thick mid-ribs add a denser texture to the dish.

ASHLIE'S DOZEN

This 'Henderson's Black Valentine' bush variety is delicious as a snap bean, but may be harvested for its rich black bean interior.

BEANS

There are so many varieties of beans in this world that I could spend the rest of my life exploring the various types to grow in our garden. That may sound like an exaggeration, but it is estimated that there are more than four hundred types of true beans in the world. I have only tried maybe ten, so I have a ways to go, but that sounds like a challenge, yeah? Though I have successfully grown a few varieties, my favorites thus far have been green beans, wax beans, soybeans, purple beans, fava beans, and butter beans. These vegetables are easy to grow and their production is prolific given the right conditions.

Bean Growth

Bean varieties are typically classified into two categories: bush beans and pole beans. Bush beans grow compact and do not require much support. These varieties may also grow between 24 and 36 inches (61 and 91 cm) in height. Pole beans grow long vines and need to be supported through either a trellis or sturdy frame. Beans of this variety can reach heights between 10 and 12 feet (3 and 3.7 m) tall. Some gardeners create archways between garden beds using cattle panels and allow pole beans to run over them. This only creates a jaw-dropping aesthetic and allows you to maximize space by growing vertically. But it is important to note that for both types of beans, you want to make sure you provide ample space for them to grow.

Because of the well-draining soil and compost that we add, beans grow well in our raised beds. Whether you are directly sowing seeds into the ground or starting seeds in trays, planting them in full sun, with a bit of 5-10-5 fertilizer (5% nitrogen, 10% phosphorus, 5% potassium), will boost their development. Also, beans are not frost-hardy, so make sure you plant them after the risk of frost has passed.

Bean Harvests

Beans are fully mature in about sixty days, and once you see that the seeds in the pods are plump they are generally ready to pick. If the seeds are too big or bulging through the pod, then they are overgrown and may not taste as good. Though many bush and pole varieties may be immediately cooked, frozen, canned, or eaten fresh, some shell bean varieties, such as dark red kidney and navy beans, require a drying period while on the plant before shelling. My favorite way to prepare beans of all sorts is either eating them fresh off the plant or pressure canning them in a homemade brine.

ASHLIE'S DOZEN

MUSTARD GREENS

There is nothing like harvesting a fresh bundle of mustard greens during the fall. This cold-weather plant produces leaves that have a sharp, tangy taste when fully developed, but younger leaves generally taste milder. Around the fall season, I typically crave warm vegetable broths and soups, and mustard greens satisfy that craving each and every time. I also have fond memories of my grandmother making a big pot of mustard greens with chopped rutabagas and turkey. She added one ingredient that just harmonized the entire pot, and that was apple cider vinegar. If you ever meet my grandmother, don't tell her I told you the secret sauce. Consuming the juice that remained from the greens (also called pot likker) was my second favorite part of the dish. Because my grandmother was from the South, many dishes were paired with either cornbread or biscuits, so that's exactly what we ate along with greens. That was good ole southern comfort food for us.

Mustard Green Growth

This vegetable is truly the gift that keeps on giving because you can chop the plant all the way to soil level, and it will continue to produce a new set of leaves. Each fall, we grow three types of mustard greens: 'Red Giant', 'Tendergreen', and 'Florida Broadleaf'. These varieties produce gigantic leaves, so even one harvest can go a long way. Since some of these varieties get so large, be sure to seed them about 6 inches (15 cm) apart and thin them out to

These leafy mustard greens (pictured on the left and right) and collard greens (pictured in the center) have the richest flavor during the colder seasons and right after a good frost.

about 12 inches (30 cm), so that they have sufficient growing space. We typically sow seeds directly into the raised beds about four weeks before the first frost and right at the turn of spring. If mustard greens are planted in warmer temperatures, the risk of bolting or flowering prematurely increases. One last advantage to growing mustard greens is the length of time it takes to go from seed to harvest, which is thirty to forty days when given loose rich soil, proper light, and consistent water. All in all, this plant is low maintenance and can make even a novice appear to be a gardening guru.

Mustard Green Harvests

Young leaves can be eaten raw as an addition to a salad or sandwich. Mature greens, which pack a spicier flavor and rougher texture, are best cooked.

ASHLIE'S DOZEN

CUCUMBERS

Cucumbers are a summertime favorite for many gardeners, because once you set out a couple of plants, you will have fruits for most of the season. This vegetable is truly meant to be eaten straight off the vine, especially the small pickling variety (which is my favorite). During the summer, my garden routine typically begins with plucking off a couple of 3- to 4-inch (7.5 to 10 cm) pickling cucumbers and slicing them for a quick snack. Their high water content and slightly sweet flavor provide me with the energy and hydration I need to get started with garden tasks, especially on a hot day.

The makings of a pickling cucumber. This variety is not only delightful pickled but also mouthwatering fresh off the vine.

Cucumber Growth

In addition to pickling cucumbers, we grow other burpless varieties, which contain smaller amounts of cucurbitacin, a compound known to cause bitterness in cucumbers and occasional indigestion in people. Burpless cucumbers like the 'English', 'Japanese', and 'Lemon' types vary in color, texture, and shape but are significantly larger than the pickling types. They also vary in flavor profile, ranging from sweet and mild to crispy and earthy.

Now I must warn you, this vegetable will take over your growing space and most, if not all, varieties should be supported on a sturdy trellis or fence. Some gardeners allow their cucumbers to grow along the ground, but I have found that trellises help keep the fruits clean and free of rot. We designed a trellis a while ago that allows our cucumber vines to grow up and over an arch in the raised bed, while the fruits dangle underneath. The cucumbers we plant each year are typically very prolific, so this method has been a creative success that makes harvesting the fruits much more efficient. Another reason why our cucumbers produce well is because we sow seeds directly into slightly acidic soil with plenty of compost after our last predicted frost date, making sure to keep the plants well-watered throughout the season. Sow the plants about 12 inches (30.5 cm) apart to allow each plant to receive the sunlight and ventilation needed to develop optimally. We pair cucumbers with other companion plants, such as chives and marigolds, to help attract pollinators and enhance fertilization of flowers for fruit production.

Cucumber Harvests

There are many varieties of cucumbers, so I recommend trying a few to see which ones you enjoy most. Some can be harvested in a small size for pickling or fresh eating (gherkins, for example), while others should be left on the vine to reach their full size. Don't let them hang on the vine for too long, though, or the skin will get tough and the fruits will be very seedy.

ASHLIE'S DOZEN

PEAS

Peas, the healthy candies of the garden. Sounds like a cruel joke and perhaps an oxymoron, but hear me when I say that their sweet, crisp flavor makes them nearly just as delicious. Because my family loves them, we grow sugar snap peas and snow peas twice a year. These peas are of the vining variety, while others, like the 'Green Arrow', are of the bush variety. While we enjoy growing the vining peas in our garden, the bush peas also produce excellent yields and are great for smaller growing spaces, like patio and container gardens.

With a shorter seed to harvest timeline, peas are some of the easiest vegetables to grow.

Pea Growth

One benefit to growing these vegetables is that they do not take long to grow—approximately sixty to seventy days to full maturation—but it's best to grow many of them to get a plentiful harvest. Though they are low maintenance and simple to grow, peas are particular about the temperatures in which they should be grown. As soon as the ground thaws from the frost in early spring or when the summer temperatures begin to cool down, we amend the soil in our raised bed with compost and an organic general-purpose fertilizer, and directly sow pea seeds. Compost feeds and keeps the soil at an ideal pH level of 6.5, while the fertilizer enhances the nutrient supply for the plants themselves. Also, because peas create a lot of vines, we typically prepare what we call a pea trellis made from twine zigzagged up and between bamboo stakes. This has worked well for the few years we have grown peas.

As recommended vegetables, peas and beans have quite a few similarities. Technically speaking, they do fall under the same taxonomy—Fabaceae—and grow in pods, but there are some major differences between the two. One difference lies in their growing condition. Peas, in contrast to beans, are best grown in temperatures that are above freezing but below 70°F (21°C). If they are grown in temperatures higher than that, their growth may be stunted and they begin to dry out. Due to their heat sensitivity, it's best to grow them in a partially shaded spot in your garden. The second major difference between peas and beans lies in their shape. The shapes of peas are generally round, while the shapes of beans vary greatly.

Pea Harvests

Whether you are growing vining or bush peas, you are bound to reap a great reward with minimal effort required. When harvest day arrives, simply give your peas a rinse, and serve them steamed as a side dish or raw with your favorite dipping sauce.

ASHLIE'S DOZEN

The crisp flavor of lettuce is enhanced when the temperatures are moderately cool.

LETTUCE

Many of us are acquainted with lettuce, including iceberg and other salad types. These varieties are some of the easiest to grow and a favorite among commercial manufacturers. While we frequently see these lettuces readily available in stores, did you know that there are approximately five groups in which lettuces may be classified? These groups include cos or romaine, crisphead, butterhead, leaf, and stem. Within these groups are many different varieties, some of which, like 'Parris Island' cos and 'Four Seasons' butterhead, are my absolute favorite to grow. There's much versatility in how these can be eaten and more importantly how they can be grown.

Lettuce Growth

While we grow our lettuce in raised beds, this vegetable does exceptionally well in hydroponic gardens. If growing outside, lettuce may be planted in early spring, as the weather during this time is not too cold and not too warm. There are some varieties of lettuce that are heat-tolerant but, generally speaking, this vegetable does not withstand temperatures above 70°F (21°C). The warmer the weather, the higher the likelihood that these plants will bolt or produce tall stalks with bitter leaves and seeds.

Lettuce is a staple in most gardens, as it is easy to grow, and the rewards are plentiful and delicious. When grown in soil rich in nitrogen and at a consistent pH of 6.5 to 7.0, most varieties will mature within fifty-five to seventy-five days. The key to successful lettuce production is maintaining the plants in partial shade with a consistent watering and fertilizing schedule. Every three weeks, we typically fertilize our lettuce plants with fish emulsion or powdered blood meal, which are both high in nitrogen. In addition, occasional pest management may be needed for these plants. Cutworms, aphids, and slugs are pretty common on these plants, but they can be addressed by simply rinsing them off with a water hose or by adding some form of organic pest repellent (such as diatomaceous earth or diluted neem oil).

Lettuce Harvests

Besides chopping up their leaves for fresh salads, I like to use lettuce as bread replacements for wraps, in soups, or sautéed for stir-fry dishes. As you experiment with growing different varieties of lettuce, I'm sure you will find many ways to prepare it for tasty meals.

ASHLIE'S DOZEN

CARROTS

Growing up, I always heard "eat your carrots if you want great vision." And there is some truth to that, as carrots possess exceptional nutritional value and are packed with essential vitamins and nutrients, such as carotenoids, which may help in preventing common eye diseases. Ever since I was younger this fact has stuck with me, and as an adult I love carrots, especially those harvested in early winter. There are so many varieties of carrots, each consisting of different shapes, lengths, and colors. I can imagine that it's hard to envision carrots being anything other than orange, but they exist in a rainbow of colors. The 'Tendersweet' carrots are tender and bright orange and pack a spectacular sweetness that is perfect for making fresh juices. The 'Black Nebula' carrots are some of the darkest carrots around, with their deep purple hue, yet they boast a rich, sweet flavor ideal for roasting. Lastly, the 'Atomic Red' carrots have a vibrant red color, comparable to watermelon, and are loaded with lycopene. This variety of carrots is fantastic raw or chopped into a hearty fall stew.

Carrots require deep, loose soil for optimal growth, and once they are ready to harvest they will pop their root tops slightly above the ground.

Carrot Growth

Similar to lettuce, carrots do not grow optimally in hot weather. Depending on your climate zone, temperatures may be ideal in the early spring, fall, and winter months, as growing carrots during these seasons typically results in sweeter flavors and richer colors. Because this is a root vegetable that does not like to be disturbed, I do not recommend starting seeds indoors and transplanting. When directly sowing seeds into the ground, one detail to consider is soil type. If you have ever tried to grow carrots and found the root to be small or deformed, you most likely experienced a soil composition issue. Carrots enjoy loose, sandy loam soil, rich in organic matter and with enough depth for their roots to grow—after all, carrots grow deep into the soil as opposed to upward. It's also important to note that the soil should be free of obstruction, meaning rocks, old roots, and balls of clay, as this can stunt carrot growth.

Carrot Harvests

Carrots take quite a bit of time to mature, so while waiting for them to grow it's best to keep their soil moist, mulched, and fed with a fertilizer high in potassium and phosphorus. In doing this you can expect to harvest your carrots after seventy to eighty days. The best part of harvesting carrots is pulling them out of the ground. We typically save this moment for when our nieces and nephews visit us for the holidays. It's a joy watching their eyes light up as they are surprised by the size of the carrot beneath the surface of the soil. With careful growing considerations and a bit of patience, carrots may become one of your favorite vegetables to grow as well.

COLLARDS

Many may agree when I say that collards are considered the greens of the South in the United States. Each year, my family and friends all across the southeast United States prepare a large pot of fresh collard greens on New Year's Eve. Some may call this an old superstition to ensure good luck and prosperity in the new year, but I consider it a savory tradition that fills my tummy on such a festive night. In southern cuisine, you will commonly see steamed or boiled collard greens prepared with some type of meat, mostly turkey or pork. The women in my family used to prepare this dish using one unique ingredient called chow chow, which was a tangy pickled vegetable relish, and boy, was it scrumptious. To this day, I cook variations of this dish with rutabagas and a few other twists.

Collard Growth

Collards are like mustard greens, in that they both thrive in the fall and winter months, and while they both belong to the *Brassica oleracea* species, collards have significant differences from mustards. If I had to describe the profile of collard greens, the flavor would be comparable to cabbage while the texture would be comparable to kale. Regarding their leaves, collards are large, dark green, and thick in texture when grown in their ideal season, and while their flavor is not as sharp as mustards, they can also possess a mild sweetness after a gentle frost. These leafy greens do well when started indoors and transplanted outside. Additionally, there is much versatility in where you can plant these greens, such as directly in the ground, in raised beds, and even in containers.

Large, thick collards have a sweet yet earthy flavor after a brief frost period. This happens due to an increase of sugars being released when temperatures drop.

The main factors for ensuring strong production are quite simple: grow in full sun with temperatures ranging from 65°F to 75°F (18.2°C to 24°C), water consistently, maintain well-draining, nutrient-rich soil fortified with organic matter (like compost), and feed with a soluble general-purpose fertilizer.

Collard Harvests

Once these main conditions have been met, you can expect to harvest your collard between fifty and sixty days after putting down your seeds. After harvesting you can either store your collards in the refrigerator for up to a week or in the freezer if you don't plan to consume them right away. If I'm not eating them as fresh collard wraps filled with other garden vegetables, then I frequently preserve our greens through canning them in a homemade brine for longer-term use. They also serve as great gifts to give to family and friends during the holiday season, and maybe even as a token of good fortune for New Year's Eve.

REAPING THE HARVEST

In developing your edible garden, you will experience rewards that are immediate and some that take a bit longer. Of course, this depends on what you define as a reward, as that is typically driven by your own intrinsic motivations. Still, gardening produces plenty of and, frequently, delicious ones. Previously, I highlighted a dozen edible plants that provide the best harvests, and within each of those plants you will find hundreds of varieties to select from. Most of the plants listed are not only straightforward to grow, but they also provide abundant harvests throughout the growing season. So, by now you may see how managing a food garden can supply you with richly diverse, nutritious, and in-season produce, but there are many more intangible goodies that may be gained along the way, such as the deeper connection to family and community and the overall gratification from accomplishing something you put your mind to.

Even though you may maintain a garden by yourself, you may find yourself wanting to share your harvests with others (whether they are human or nonhuman). I know of few gardeners who can resist the urge to care for family, neighbors, and colleagues with their bountiful harvests, and honestly that's what stewards do. Yet, in that exchange of fresh foods, a deeper connection to people is cultivated as well. People bond over great food, and

Homegrown tomatoes are known to be delectable right off the vine, but roasted with freshly picked herbs is flavor reimagined.

when you are able to take care of the community around you, the reward may lie in the contribution that you are making to the well-being of the collective. As for the gratification that comes with gardening and growing food, I don't know anyone who was born with that knowledge—it takes time, intention, and consistency to develop that skill. This concept is similar to the life cycle of a seed, which can't become a productive plant without going through a process. Therefore, once you learn how to grow your food, the lush harvests that you will reap may evoke a sense of achievement and greater self-actualization that you can indeed do something beyond what you perceive your capabilities to be.

WORTH THE WAIT

There are many aesthetically pleasing and delicious plants to grow, and I have covered only a few of the thousands that are available. In a world that moves fast with desires often being obtained quickly, gardening encourages many of us to slow down and appreciate the fact that good things don't always come fast. As we've gone along, you can see that cultivating a garden takes a significant amount of effort and time. From the time required for planning and researching best growing techniques, to choosing seeds and waiting for them to produce, you may wonder whether gardening and growing your own

After sixty to ninety days, this sweet yellow bell pepper has ripened on the bush and is ready for harvesting. Pepper plants are prolific producers, so you can expect an average of seven to ten peppers per plant.

food is even worth the wait. Allow me to reveal why good things, like fresh garden-grown foods, may be worth waiting for.

Have you ever been out running errands and you weighed the option of purchasing something quick from a fast-food restaurant or cooking something from scratch at home? If you have, you may find that sometimes fast food doesn't quite satisfy the way a good cooked meal with homegrown produce does. Most of the time when you buy fast foods or commercially available foods, you are unaware of how the food was made and the process and timeline for how it got to your plate. However, with growing an edible garden, you are the producer of your own food, and therefore you have more control of the ground-to-table pipeline. Growing your own food will undoubtedly require significantly more time to produce, but you will know where your food comes from and exactly how it was made because you were present for it all. The effort put into growing your food will lend greater value and meaning to what you are consuming, and it will taste even better.

I remember in my first year of gardening, I explored growing the large and sweet 'Kellogg's Breakfast' tomato plants from seed. I was so excited to watch the evolution of these plants from the moment they germinated to the time of harvest. More specifically, I was motivated to wait for some of the tomatoes to completely ripen right on the vine. I knew that there were no harmful substances on this plant at any point, so watching the fruits ripen untreated allowed me to appreciate the fullness of such natural processes. Furthermore, I could trust that what I would soon taste was the real unadulterated form of the produce. So, this elicited not only appreciation, but also a balanced sense of accomplishment and undeniable joy. Once I was finally able to taste the fruit after waiting over ninety days, the flavor was unlike anything that I had tasted from fast-food vendors or big-box stores, and I was able to harvest copious amounts of tomatoes all throughout the season.

As you can see, gardening as a whole, but especially edible gardening, teaches you to slow down

My grandmother once told me, "When you love what you grow, what you love grows."

and examine the source and quality of what you are growing. There is one more thing that you may find waiting helps you appreciate, and that's yourself. Remember the sense of accomplishment I previously mentioned? Well, you will gain a sense of pride at all that has developed within yourself as you learned to grow something that is good for you and perhaps those around you. The wait will teach you greater patience as you observe the gradual development of your plants from seed to full maturity. This wait will also teach you perseverance, which you will gain as you push through and troubleshoot challenges. And we can't forget about hope, as this is the root of why someone chooses to wait in the first place. Hope will keep you content along the journey, while excited and focused on the prize. Ultimately, through gardening you learn to relinquish control of time and make a truce with it.

If you have walked with me this far on our journey, I have no doubt that you will find the waiting process for growing the foods that you desire and deserve to be worth every minute and every bit of effort.

Next page: A large 'Kellogg's Breakfast' tomato sitting among other unique heirloom tomatoes.

PERSPECTIVES OF A GARDENER

Meet Misilla dela Llana
Location: Washington State
Social Media Handle: @learntogrow

MY GARDENING JOURNEY

I wasn't aware of it as a child, but my mother naturally instilled the art and cultivation of plants in me when I was young. When we moved to the United States from the Philippines, I remember her planting and maintaining flower beds that flourished with carnations, tulips, daffodils, and fragrant roses. My family and I helped pull weeds and water plants, and we had fun foraging for white clovers for their sweet ambrosia. Back then, clover proliferated throughout many lawns and was considered a rampant weed, although they provide an excellent source of nectar for the bees. Looking back, this memory helped me understand the harmony that occurs within nature between organisms. And though I was unfamiliar with many gardening concepts during that time, over the years I quite naturally developed a strong affinity for gardening.

Misilla in front of her Washington home garden on a bright and warm day.

MOTIVATION TO BEGIN

Later on in my life, my mother continued to encourage me to garden by gifting plants on several occasions. When I moved into my first apartment, gardening became a hobby and I started with a few herbs and several houseplants. Over the years, the act of gardening continued as my husband and I grew our own family. We had the opportunity to start a container garden with our children on the balcony of our condo, and were able to grow tomatoes, peppers, strawberries, lettuce, herbs, and spinach. And presently, we maintain several in-ground and raised beds, as well as some plants in containers filled with edible crops, herbs, flowers, and ornamental varieties. So, as you can see, gardening has been an evolution for me, and has in many ways been a part of my life since I was a young child.

EDIBLE GARDENING AND FOOD SOVEREIGNTY

When my family lived in the Philippines, food (especially nutritious types) wasn't always easy to come by due to unstable access, inadequate infrastructure, and the occurrence of

Misilla's garden consists of a mixture of metal raised beds and containers mindfully positioned to enhance the environment around her.

natural calamities. Though the Philippines is full of land prime for agricultural development, these barriers often have detrimental effects on the food supply. So, there were many times that we relied on the fruit trees and wild edible plants that grew near our home. To have access to wholesome and fresh food, and control over what we eat, is what I consider having food sovereignty. The very opportunity to produce our own food is empowering and liberating.

It is my belief that gardening and growing food is a lifestyle, and this lifestyle has taught me countless lessons while improving my overall health, both physically and emotionally. When we grow our own food, we're not only nourishing our bodies, but we also help to sustain the ecosystem that surrounds us. Gardening is beneficial to my overall well-being and keeps me grounded. It helps me gain a more positive and gratifying outlook on life.

HOW GARDENING INFLUENCES MY PERSPECTIVE ON FOOD AND THE ENVIRONMENT

Ever since I started an edible garden, vegetables, fruits, and herbs have never tasted so good! I have found that homegrown food is not only significantly more flavorful and perhaps more nutritious, but it is sustainable, convenient, cost-saving, and intrinsically rewarding. Growing food at home allows me to cultivate the quantity of my choosing and food free from harmful chemicals. Furthermore, my family and I have sought to cultivate our property with quite a few native plants, such as red huckleberry, Oregon grape, and black elderberry, as well as maple, Douglas fir, and hemlock trees. I also now understand how this natural vegetation on our property contributes to the well-being of our environment by maintaining soil health, reducing water runoff from precipitation, and providing food and habitats for wildlife. Gradually, we have incorporated native flowers, shrubs, and herbs to further enhance the biodiversity of our garden, which will help restore and preserve local ecosystems for generations.

EMPOWERED TO GROW NEW FOODS

Some of the selections of foods that I grow were unique vegetables and fruits passed down from relatives. While I frequently seek to try out new and rare varieties of foods, I thoroughly enjoy growing many of the common vegetables and fruits as well. I typically strive to plant crops that my family loves, and those that perform well in my climate. Additionally, perennial types of produce that can be harvested year-round are particularly valuable in my garden. I am a strong advocate for having access to homegrown food year-round, and learning how to do so is what I teach about in my book, *Four-Season Food Gardening: How to Grow Vegetables, Fruits, and Herbs Year-Round.*

Aside from cultivating popular types such as tomatoes, leafy greens, legumes, carrots, and squash, I occasionally experiment with unique varieties that are typically grown outside of my region, but compatible with my local ecosystem. Gardening has taught me much about plants, soil, and the environment. I've learned that it is conceivable to grow beyond regional limitations by harnessing the proper resources and applying the knowledge that is gained over time. The possibilities for food can be endless!

A vibrant basket of garlic scapes, crisp lettuce, peas, raspberries, and edible flowers produced by Misilla's garden.

CHAPTER 5

EMPOWERMENT THROUGH GROWING

Reclaiming Your Food Authority

When reflecting upon the term "reclaim," quite often it's assumed that something has been stolen and there is a need to get it back. Generally, this term carries with it a burden of wrongdoing or something undesirable, and honestly, that very well may be the case in many circumstances. But how do you reclaim something that you've never had in the first place? Upon exploring the meaning a bit more, Merriam-Webster dictionary defines "reclaim" as making something available for human use by changing natural conditions. This definition does not assume what you have or don't have; it simply highlights the act of making provision and making something accessible. This is profound because it gets at the heart of why becoming a gardener and growing your food can indeed be a form of reclamation, where you are reclaiming your autonomy to feed your body what it needs to optimally sustain life. As we go along in this chapter, I will cover topics such as how edible gardening reshapes our perception of food, redefines good food, and allows us to forge healthier relationships with food, all of which may further embolden you to seek your own path toward reclaiming your access to better food options.

Opposite: There is something incredibly empowering about being a part of the development of your food, like watching this 'Purple Moon' kale plant move from seed to ground to table.

A garden has the ability to produce nearly all of your nutritious needs, from herbs to fruits to vegetables.

In general, most people begin to develop their perception of food when they are babies or young children. After all, that is when food preferences and dietary habits begin to form. And this is typically a result of the types of foods they interact with and what they learn in their environment. Furthermore, depending on your environment, culture, and even genetic makeup, your experience with certain foods can influence what you perceive as the best foods for you. In turn, this preference forms the basis of the dietary habits that generally stick with you well into adulthood—that is, unless you gradually adapt them. However, many people do not adapt or make adjustments to their dietary habits unless they are either prompted to or have found that something is missing nutritionally. And right there lie the reasons why edible gardens may help supplement or enhance diets and food preferences, no matter your age.

The way we perceive food is based upon many factors, but more specifically how we have interacted with food based upon our senses. Interestingly, cultivating a garden also allows us to interact with and perceive food throughout its full development using all five of our senses: seeing, touching, tasting, smelling, and hearing. It is common for most people to use all of their senses when consuming any type of food, but it is especially unique to be able to utilize all of your senses as you cultivate and watch fresh food undergo its full evolution from seed to table. Incredible, yeah? As a result, growing your own food can gradually adapt your food preferences, while further influencing what you consider good food to be.

In this manner, gardening has the potential to clarify and redefine what you consider to be "good" food. When you think of what good food is, you may associate it with meals that have brought you satisfaction and immediate comfort. There are most often good memories attached to these foods and you are likely to recall what they smell, taste, and look

Being able to witness where your food comes from makes eating it all the more enjoyable.

In southern parts of the United States, sautéed crookneck squash, 'Nero de Milano' zucchini, and Vidalia onions make a savory side dish to nearly any meal.

The food produced in your garden has the ability to influence your perception of "good" food.

Chives, or *Allium schoenoprasum*, are aromatic herbs that feed the pollinators with the nectar in their flowers and offer a steady supply of delicious culinary seasonings.

Opposite: As a gardener, you have the ability to be the consumer and the producer of the food you need to thrive.

like. And even the thought of these meals may warm your heart and stir your appetite. But, oftentimes what you may associate with good food may not be the best food for your overall health and wellness. For example, a scoop of ice cream may be delicious to the tongue and mind after a gratifying and savory meal, but if you're lactose intolerant, or allergic to dairy like me, that gratification is short-lived and suffering typically comes within thirty minutes. This example can be applied to your perception of good food. Just because your preferences say that a particular food is delicious does not automatically mean that it is good for you in the long run. This is relevant to the topic of growing your food because you are able to interact with a variety of nutritious, visually appealing, and good-tasting food items that stimulate all of your senses.

So, imagine with me for a moment, walking into your garden on a warm spring day and seeing different types of vegetables, herbs, and fruits growing all around you on bushes and vines. As you walk around you can hear the melodies of the wind chimes and birds singing. You rub a few herb plants and the smell of fennel, chives, and rosemary fills the air. You turn slightly toward your vibrant multicolored tomatoes, grab a fruit, and bite into it as its sweet juices pour into your mouth. While continuing around your garden tasting and touching more vegetables and fruits, you can hear the crunches and crisps of every food item you bite into. And after eating just enough to feel full, you are completely satisfied and in bliss that all of this nutritious food is yours whenever you need it. Ultimately, these food garden experiences encourage curiosity and help forge healthier relationships with food.

In some modern societies, you will see that many prefer quick food items that can keep them going through the hustle and bustle of life. Trust me, I've been there and understand it. But in this evolution of societies becoming hyperfocused on productivity, there appears to be a disconnect in the relationship that many have with food. Many people are often unable to use all of their senses to truly understand what they are eating and where it comes from. What makes food good is often convoluted, and unfortunately you may see this obscurity manifested in health outcomes. So it makes you wonder, how can you have a healthy relationship with something you don't fully know?

Now, I also have to highlight an alternative concept that contributes greatly to forming a healthy relationship with food, and that is balance. Good food should neither cause pain nor evoke apathy and feel like punishment. Furthermore, it is my belief that food is holistic and should be aligned with every aspect of you, including your body, your culture, and your values. Gardening not only encourages you to seek greater understanding of your food and its source, but it also inspires you to be curious about foods you have never tried, which further expands how you perceive food. All in all, growing a diverse edible garden can redefine how you view what is good for you and strengthen your relationship with food—even the occasional ice cream.

Thymus vulgaris, commonly known as thyme, is a fragrant, low-growing perennial that is frequently used fresh and dried in culinary dishes.

Red-veined sorrel is a unique perennial leafy green that looks vibrant in the garden and is best when harvested young and eaten fresh.

EDUCATIONAL EMPOWERMENT

I walked you through how edible gardens can enhance our perception of and relationship with food and you may have understood that there's a degree of learning that will also take place as you seek to reclaim your food. At the beginning of the chapter I discussed the concept of reclamation, and how you can make provision for or access to something by changing natural conditions. However, in order to do this, you have to know what you need to change to create that access for yourself. This is where educational empowerment comes in, and I am not talking only about academic education. This empowerment through learning pertains to the knowledge that you may grow and share as you go along your gardening journey. More specifically, some of those opportunities for education will center on learning food varieties and their benefits, nurturing your environment while growing food, and receiving enlightenment on the history of the foods you grow. So, let's see what's in store, shall we?

I am going to kick off by telling you a quick story of how I was taught to appreciate tomatoes. Okay, I know, it's crazy, because I have referenced tomatoes many times throughout this book. However, I like to frequently use myself as an example to highlight that I was not always a nutritionally focused gardener. Like you, I had to go through the process of becoming a more informed steward of my body and my environment. Be that as it may, I grew up despising tomatoes. The texture, smell, look, and taste repulsed me, and believe or not I couldn't even get my body to ingest them.

Now, I must interject that my experience has always been with the big red store-bought tomatoes. But each year, I made attempts to try these

It's never too early or too late to learn how to garden.

tomatoes to no avail—until I started gardening. I didn't want to give up on trying to consume tomatoes, so I researched different varieties that could potentially address why I didn't like them, and interestingly I found several. After growing them, I learned that it wasn't that I didn't like tomatoes, I just had limited access to more varieties—and possibly healthier varieties. I perceived tomatoes to only be red, heavily seeded, and bland, not orange, citrusy, and flavorful. The world of food is vast, and there are many ways to prepare it. Educating yourself on different food varieties can open up greater access to not just more food, but perhaps even higher-quality food. Moreover, the experience I highlighted goes beyond tomatoes, as it applies to many more produce items that can be grown right in your garden. Through challenging yourself to explore more food

The diversity of food that the garden provides can change your perception of a food you considered to be unappetizing, thus making space for new good food memories.

Gardening will expose you to many diverse flavors of some of the most common vegetables and fruits. For instance, this 'Sun Gold' cherry tomato has an intense fruity flavor.

Sometimes all it takes is exploring different varieties of a food item in order to change your perspective. Tomatoes are now some of my favorite fruits to consume.

This spaghetti squash plant produces vines that grow up to 8 feet (2.4 m) in length, and can yield up to five fruits per plant.

The triple-octagon-shaped bed that we refer to as "octa-garden" consists of more than sixty medicinal and culinary plants that we cultivated for the health of ourselves and the health of the local ecosystem.

varieties, you may begin to enjoy certain food items that you have never tried or once strongly disliked.

One thing about the concept of education is that rarely will you see what is learned remaining bottled up within the individual. The same applies to gardening, in that as you learn more about your garden and what foods you can grow, there will be an intrinsic motivation or urge to share that knowledge with others—and funnily enough, you will find that many will enjoy it. Sharing your knowledge with others is also important as it helps them connect the dots within their own food journey. For instance, have you ever walked through a garden and saw a vegetable or fruit item that looked familiar or like something you frequently ate, but you had never seen it growing in its natural element? It's a mind-blowing moment because there is almost an enlightenment that takes place and a deeper understanding of the origin of a food that seemed so common and familiar.

Now, imagine being able to usher someone else into a similar revelation through your garden. As a gardener, you will have the opportunity to teach others the benefits of certain edible plants, which can also help them realize how particular foods may be good for them. This is also where I believe the dietitians and nutrition professionals come into play, as they provide tailored guidance on food options that you may consider based upon your specific health needs and goals. Educating yourself on best food-growing practices and sharing that knowledge with others is key to strengthening the collective and making greater strides in nurturing the environment.

The essence of empowerment is developing an ability, and when it comes to the environment, this is often either overlooked or misunderstood. You may be curious about what the environment should have the ability to do, and I would simply say that the environment should have the ability to thrive, just as we desire the same for ourselves. I also recognize that this concept is complex, like the issue of food security that I touched on earlier. I believe that the first step in healing the earth is by starting in your own backyard. So, envision if many people were to do just that. A series of small actions over time can lead to a big impact.

Without a healthy environment, there is no healthy garden. In order to develop, maintain, and produce the edible goodness that will come out of your green haven, your space needs to be a haven for nature as well. Remember, as a gardener you are a steward, and the ways in which you maintain your garden and grow your food may have direct effects on the environment around you. As you think about how your garden may contribute to your wellness, perhaps consider how it may also contribute to the wellness of other organisms and life forms around you, as they too are part of the collective.

In previous chapters, I have covered the importance of many natural elements that define and contribute to the prosperity of a garden, but as you walk your own gardening path, you will certainly desire to learn more. Fortunately, there are many easily accessible educational resources in the form of books, blogs, websites, social media, and local agricultural agencies that can guide you on how to effectively nurture the environment around you as you learn to grow your food. Additionally, depending on your environment, these resources may even lead to learning more about the history of the foods you grow.

Herbs like yarrow, Chinese motherwort, sage, and lemon balm play a major role in providing food and shelter to beneficial insects and pollinators.

The unique thing about educating yourself on diverse food varieties is that you gain the opportunity to learn where they originated. Food, especially what you can grow, has a historical footprint that can be traced through generational stories and even genetic testing. When gardening, you will be given access (either for free or at a low cost) to thousands of seeds that, when cultivated properly, can produce the same fruits and vegetables that were seen, touched, smelled, tasted, and heard by gardeners of centuries past. This is particularly important in the conversation of culturally relevant foods, as many of these growers of the past may have been your ancestors. And this, my friend, is the heart of reclaiming a food that you may have never been able to access.

In summary, knowledge is powerful. There is power in learning how your food impacts you, there is liberation in connecting others to the knowledge you have gained, there is honor in understanding the history of your food, and there is privilege in being able to seek out more than what is presented to you.

Page 132: The joy of gardening is multiplied when we are able to share the passion and knowledge with others.

Gardening will teach you to value and appreciate every organism you share space with.

Amaranthus cruentus, or red amaranth, can grow up to 6 feet (1.8 m) tall and produces grains and leaves that are highly nutritious staple foods in Asia, the West Indies, India, and Africa.

Like many other chile peppers, the jalapeño pepper is a staple in Mexican culture and cuisine. Though they are commonly harvested in their green state, their spicy flavor increases as they turn red.

It's one thing to be able to grow healthy food for yourself, but it's another thing to teach the next generation how to do the same. This is how communities are strengthened.

GROWING THOSE AROUND YOU

The final aspect of being an empowered gardener is putting greater intentionality behind growing the people around you. This doesn't necessarily mean that you have to feverishly scope out people to teach, as that is quite the pressure and could take away from the joys of gardening. What this simply encourages you to do is lean into gardening with the heart to serve and learn from others. Sometimes it's easy to assume that as you are contributing to others' growth, you are in the teaching role; however, that couldn't be further from the truth, as growing others isn't always about teaching them. Most of the time you are learning from them through compassion and empathy.

I would like to believe that compassion and empathy are common traits for gardeners; after all, they are nurturers, right? Over the course of becoming a gardener, you will be presented with opportunities to show your compassion as you help others understand the value of gardening and nutritious, homegrown foods. But it's important to recognize that not everyone will view gardening the way you do, possibly due to fear, feelings of inadequacy, or simply it just not being their cup of tea. However, it helps to apply empathy in understanding that just like you, everyone undergoes their own journey in learning the value of food, and it varies in time and effort. As a result of your kindness, you may find that people feel more compelled to learn what you know and grow right along with you. And if you spread this compassion around, next thing you know, you are helping to strengthen your community. Chef Yotan Ottolenghi said it best: "Food can unite. Food can bring people together in a way nothing else could."

As I have gone through how gardening fosters empowerment within you, it's not difficult to see how this can also permeate your community. The mere act of gardening and sharing fresh homegrown foods promotes greater social connections, strengthens communities, and builds self-reliance. It doesn't matter whether you are an introvert or an

Harvesting fresh food and herbs has a way of piquing the interest of even the youngest of us.

extrovert, as I'm sure that you value genuine connection with others. Gardening will help you connect with people in a deeper and more meaningful way, especially if they happen to be working alongside you in the garden. You may experience some of the best conversations while planting seedlings or pulling weeds.

In addition to fostering stronger connections, gardening provides practical lessons on how to become more self-reliant. You now know what this looks like on an individual level, but how about on the community level? If people work together to grow gardens or share food with one another from their individual gardens, the fundamental needs of the collective can be met. Through hard work and resourcefulness, you and others in your community may become more cognizant of the needs of others, especially the most vulnerable in your community. You may feel empowered enough to generate the supplies, including food, that are needed to sustain yourselves as a community. It is through gardening that people are able to unite over communal tasks and, of course, good food.

Seeking to grow others requires a great deal of growth within yourself, from developing compas-

sion and patience to building an empathetic heart. Making yourself available to guide others on how to cultivate their own gardens and grow their own food can be one of the most rewarding experiences for not just you, but also the recipient. It provides a way to build potentially long-lasting relationships with family, colleagues, or neighbors.

As you move forward as an empowered gardener, there are a few key recommendations that I will provide for your reflection. The first is to focus on being a good example, not a perfect one. There is no such thing as a perfect gardener, and there is no perfect way to garden. Any good lesson you learn along the way will be valuable for yourself and potentially for others. However, just as much as you are willing to grow others, be equally, if not more, willing to learn from others, as this too helps others grow. And finally, never stop increasing your knowledge of gardening best practices, different foods to grow, and how to be a better steward. The more you know, the more you grow, and the more you share with those around you.

Next page: Gardeners take joy in sharing what is grown, whether it be food or knowledge.

PERSPECTIVES OF A GARDENER

Meet Deanna Talerico
Location: California
Social Media Handle: @deannacat3
Website: homesteadandchill.com

MY GARDENING JOURNEY

I have been gardening for over a decade now. I began casually gardening in 2007 while I was in college but became a far more passionate and involved gardener when my husband and I bought our first home in 2013.

Quite frankly, I wouldn't be who I am today without gardening! It has become so much more than just a fun hobby for me. It's a lifestyle, one that nourishes my mind, body, and spirit. In addition to the obvious health benefits of eating fresh organic foods, gardening keeps me active and enhances my ability to problem-solve and think critically. It has also taught me a thing or two about patience, gratitude, and second chances. I feel most happy and less stressed when I am outside with my hands in the dirt, fresh air and sunshine on my face, and connecting with nature. Even more, gardening has become something special and rewarding that my husband and I can enjoy together. I think many people underestimate the power of gardening until they engage in it and feel it for themselves. It truly is therapy!

MOTIVATION TO BEGIN

I started my first little raised bed garden while I was in college. At the time, I was studying environmental studies and was quite involved with various sustainability programs on campus. Being a part of that atmosphere and learning about how beneficial organic farming practices and local food systems are to our environment, I was

Deanna standing with vegetable seedlings that are ready for transplanting into her garden beds.

Deanna's garden has been carefully curated to be a welcoming space to various beneficial organisms.

inspired to try growing some of my own food at home while exploring composting techniques. Also, during this time, I had just recently lost my dad to kidney cancer, so I was reflecting a lot on how our eating habits, environmental exposures, and lifestyle choices are so intimately tied to health outcomes.

EDIBLE GARDENING AND FOOD SOVEREIGNTY

I recognize that I am really fortunate in that I've always had the access and ability to purchase a variety of fresh foods. Nevertheless, gardening has given me more freedom of choice over the quality and variety of foods we eat in our household. More recently, especially in the time of the pandemic, we have felt even more secure by being able to meet some of our basic needs right at home.

Firecider, which is Deanna's special homemade medicinal tonic, is made with various produce grown right in her garden.

I feel an even deeper sense of freedom through gardening now that it has become my full-time job. For several years now, my husband and I have successfully owned and operated Homestead and Chill, a popular gardening and natural health blog and shop. Through our business, we teach and inspire others to grow their own food, compost at home, care for pollinators and wildlife, preserve food and prepare healthy meals, and make natural body care products for themselves. This work has been incredibly rewarding, knowing that it helps others achieve a higher level of freedom too, including enhancing their direct access to fresh food, as well as the mental and spiritual benefits that come along with gardening and self-sufficiency. Through gardening, I've found my purpose, and am grateful to have the freedom to do what I love for work.

HOW GARDENING INFLUENCES MY PERSPECTIVE ON FOOD AND THE ENVIRONMENT

Gardening has greatly deepened my appreciation for both food and the environment. It's one thing to learn about natural ecosystems, nutrient-dense foods, and regenerative/organic farming in a textbook, but it's something else entirely to actively participate in it. Sowing the tiniest of seeds that transform into bountiful food on your plate, observing pollinators and other beneficial insects hard at work, and turning your own food waste into free fertilizer is simply amazing. I'm honored to play a role in fostering a healthy ecosystem within my own yard, and I have a deeper respect for farmers and farm laborers who dedicate their efforts and resources to this as well. Last but not least, the connection I have with my own food encourages me to reflect upon the state of my country's food systems and environmental perils. However, I remain hopeful by doing my part to encourage others to start gardening to promote greater impact in the fight for a more sustainable food system and environment.

EMPOWERED TO GROW NEW FOODS

I have enjoyed growing so many things! Gardening is fantastic in how it pushes you to grow, in more ways than one. At first, I grew some of the common vegetables like tomatoes, zucchini, and peppers. But over time I felt inspired to try to grow more unique foods: turmeric, pineapple guava, cucamelons, lemongrass, passionfruit, leeks, romanesco, and kohlrabi. Through growing my own food, I have been able to grow a plethora of interesting heirloom varieties that are not commonly found in stores. Believe it or not, there are thousands of varieties of vegetables and fruits to select from. Beyond food, I've enjoyed learning how to grow herbs and flowers to use in medicinal teas, tinctures, and homemade body care products. Coming full circle, gardening encourages us to constantly try new recipes and preservation methods to ensure that none of our homegrown produce goes to waste—before it hits the compost, that is!

The best foods possess a rainbow of colors, like this wide harvest spread from Deanna's backyard garden.

CHAPTER 6

FREEDOM THROUGH FOOD

The Power of Homegrown Food for Holistic Wellness

Over the years there has been a growing interest in the benefits of homegrown food, not just for greater access to fresh options, but also for the holistic wellness benefits. I emphasize wellness as opposed to simply health because it encompasses all of the many dimensions of a person. In short, "health" refers to the state of your physical, mental, and social well-being, while "wellness" refers to the active process you undergo to enhance or maintain balance in all of the areas of your well-being. Such areas may include the physical, emotional, spiritual, social, intellectual, environmental, and even occupational aspects of you, but in this time together, I will highlight a select few. Earlier on, I briefly discussed a few areas of well-being that gardening and growing your own food may improve, and as we continue forward, I will cover in greater detail how growing food may enhance your overall wellness. On that, let's dive specifically into the benefits of growing food for your physical well-being.

Opposite: The manual labor required to set up and maintain your garden will certainly provide you with an opportunity to exercise and get the blood flowing—both are key for optimal health.

Next page: Paul Prudhomme, an extraordinary Cajun chef, once said, "You don't need a silver fork to eat good food."

Colorful produce, like this homegrown purple cabbage, packs a significant amount of the antioxidants, vitamins, and nutrients that your body may need and perhaps craves.

EXERCISE AND PHYSICAL WELLNESS

At this point, you are most likely aware of all of the appealing and mouthwatering food you can grow using whatever space you deem a garden: foods like crunchy purple cabbage, sweet golden bell peppers, crispy pickling cucumbers, and juicy sun-ripened tomatoes all growing in abundance. You may be aware that your body relies on essential vitamins and nutrients to function optimally, and without the recommended intake of these items, you can potentially experience health challenges. Fortunately, gardens, when cultivated properly and consistently, will produce foods that may help supplement many of the essential vitamins and nutrients that your body needs and may even crave from day to day. This consistent access to foods that you need can maintain and possibly transform your physical well-being.

In addition to the nutritional advantages, growing food (well, gardening in general) promotes greater movement and exercise. Many gardeners will agree when I say that you can get a whole-body workout in your garden, as you haul rocks and soil in a wheelbarrow and leave the garden panting and drenched in sweat. No matter the size of your space, carrying soil, squatting to sow seeds, reaching to prune plants, and hauling baskets of produce require a bit of labor that can translate into healthy body movement in your major muscle groups. Though some of these activities can vary in intensity, there are others that are just strenuous enough to make you break a little sweat and feel a gentle burn in your muscles. An added benefit is that you have the power to regulate the intensity of your garden workout, all while getting tasks done around your space. All things considered, growing an edible garden is practically a double win that affords you both balanced workouts and balanced food as the rewards.

Tending to my garden brings peace to my mind, while growing wholesome food nourishes my body and my soul. This is the essence of food freedom.

MENTAL AND SPIRITUAL WELLNESS

In addition to the physical benefits, there are some generous mental and spiritual health perks that come with gardening. Now, I want to pause and acknowledge that these domains of health are not quite as concrete as the physical health domain, meaning they can be subjective to the person. However, I encourage you to consider these domains equally important to all other domains within the scope of wellness. But whether you experience none or all of these benefits, all is well because these are completely based upon your individual needs and autonomous gardening journey.

Growing food can help your mental and spiritual health by inspiring you to practice mindfulness, boosting your mood and promoting a greater connection to nature. As you continue your gardening journey, you may find that the very essence of plants has a remarkable way of inviting you to stop and focus on what you see in the present moment. This phenomenon is fascinating because many of us have at least a hundred thoughts racing through our minds at any given minute. Yet when in the presence of green life, the speed of those thoughts seems to decrease until you find yourself grounded, quiet, and at peace, even for a moment. A similar experience can be felt while observing and caring for the food-producing plants in your garden.

There are many stressors that you may face from day to day, which can leave you anxious and even weary. Research evidence shows that managing a garden may have positive effects on your mental and emotional health. The act of simply walking around your garden, observing, and nibbling on the various vegetables and fruits growing can easily lift your mood after a long and tough day. Even in the mundane tasks, you may find ways to center your mind using practices such as prayer, mindfulness, or even nothing at all. Regardless of how you find balance, gardening can promote greater connectedness to nature and the things around you, all while feeding your mind, body, and spirit. Being out in nature can also transform your perspective on yourself and the world around you. Fortunately, this transformation tends to be rooted in greater insight, respect, and appreciation.

With all of the many successes that the garden brings, there are also the challenges. Nonetheless, it's in both of these experiences that you may find a more balanced way of thinking. You may find value in the challenges just as much as you do the wins because you will recognize that both carry lessons for becoming a better gardener. Likewise, it's in that balanced place that you may also gain clarity around your role in this world, and perhaps even your purpose. Although that sounds hyperbolic, it happens quite frequently. Gardening can boost your capacity for joy and reaffirm a more positive and healthy perspective of yourself, your relationship with food, and your capabilities.

When nurturing something so fundamental as a seed, and taking time to research and care for it as it develops, you may discover characteristics and talents within yourself that may not be exhibited or utilized in other aspects of your life. Without a doubt, this aspect can be one of the most freeing experiences as you learn much about yourself. Where you may feel you are not very creative, you may find yourself vividly imagining, designing, and building an exquisite green sanctuary from scratch. Or perhaps you may not be used to expressing gentleness and sensitivity, yet you may find yourself delicately caring for the flowers and feeding the butterflies and bumblebees. Through gardening, you may also find that there is an aspect of yourself that is untapped and waiting to be free. It may be an aspect of yourself that is not defined by your aesthetics, occupation, or social status—it's an element in you so fundamental, like the seed, yet authentic. And your garden is the space that brings it to life. Sounds lovely, right?

There is always something to do in the garden, but even the most mundane tasks can ease the mind and wash away the worries of the heart.

Growing various medicinal herbs is yet another step toward self-sufficiency and may further support health and wellness within yourself and even your garden.

Artichokes can take up to four months to develop and when they mature, you can either harvest a hearty vegetable or let it be and observe its elaborate bright purple flower. In either phase, you can't help but appreciate its many cycles.

Watching a seed develop into food for my family elicits immeasurable joy and pride and a deep sense of awareness of what we are truly capable of achieving.

COMMUNITY WELLNESS

Lastly, wellness doesn't stop at the individual—after all, many individuals make up a community, and the wellness of the community is just as important. As I highlighted in chapter 5, edible gardens can boost resilience, camaraderie, and compassion within communities, but changes on this level have to start with the actions of individuals like you. When building and maintaining a garden, you will gradually find yourself becoming not just a steward of your space, but also a steward of other spaces you enter and the living beings you encounter. The small changes that take place within you can directly and indirectly affect those around you and within your community, and I will share a small yet liberating experience that I have encountered that highlights how this may be so.

In my first few years of gardening, I realized the many differences in seeds: how they came in all shapes and sizes, and even the rate at which they matured varied. I also recognized that I did not have to program or create the seeds, as they pretty much possessed everything they needed to grow into whatever fruit, herb, or vegetable they were designed to be. My responsibility was to learn their characteristics,

do my best to provide what they needed to thrive, and respect what they were going to develop into. Some of these plants even produced food that I had never tried before, but ultimately all produced foods that contributed to healthier meals for my household and the overall prosperity of the garden. Their differences are what made the garden extraordinary.

This example translates to the community, because just as there are many different types of seeds and plants, so are there many different types of people. Gardening, if you allow it, may help you understand the value in learning, nurturing, and respecting those around you with all of their differences and for who they are purposed to be. Now, imagine for a moment if other empowered individuals in your community acted similarly. This level of respect and stewardship for another can go a long way and lead to enhanced health, increased morale, and greater resilience of communities. This is the spirit of freedom through food. So you see, growing your own food is not just defying the status quo in your food system, but it is also a reclamation of your freedom to eat well, live well, and be well.

A bowl of multicolored bell peppers—all with different flavor profiles and rates of maturation. Yet it is their differences that make this bowl nutritionally rich and give it culinary depth.

Food has the power to heal and unite—all you need are plates, serving spoons, and a readiness to indulge in good food.

Garden-to-table is not just a movement about food. It is an empowered and sustainable lifestyle that can give you greater control of what you allow in your body and on your plate.

HISTORY OF GARDEN-TO-TABLE

We often hear the term "garden-to-table," but have you ever thought about where this concept comes from? Technically speaking, the idea of growing food in a home garden is not new, as it has been taking place in many households and communities all around the world for centuries. As a matter of fact, home gardens were such an obvious necessity that they were rarely viewed as something remarkable. Yet over the past few decades, there has been increasing interest in growing food at home, especially in the United States, thus transforming garden-to-table from a mere concept into an explosive and liberating movement.

To provide you with a bit of history on how this movement began, I will highlight a few events that took place, starting with the victory gardens. During World War I, agricultural production in Europe took a major loss, as many farmers were recruited for military service and their farms were destroyed in the war. As the United States and other countries joined in the fight, there was an increasing burden to feed allies, civilians, and those fighting on the front lines due to food shortages. Then, a wealthy entrepreneur by the name of Charles Lathrop Pack assembled the National War Garden to motivate Americans to grow and store fresh foods that could be exported to allies. Now, remember when I explained how people unite over food? Well, that's exactly what happened here. By 1942, nearly 15 million people came together under a common goal and began transforming vacant lots, yards, and school grounds into what eventually became known as "victory gardens." Close to 20 million gardens were constructed and produced approximately 8 million tons of fresh, nutritionally rich food. Though this movement continued until the end of World War I, it left a lasting global impression and eventually reemerged during World War II.

As you can see, it is easy to understand how impactful the victory gardens were during times of war and global hardships. After all, these spaces served as sources of sustenance and successful symbols of hope, empowerment, and humanity during tumultuous times. Yet, this influx in food autonomy didn't remain as solely a wartime intervention. Over time, it evolved into a mission of freedom that addressed deficiencies in national and local food systems. And that mission led to the farm-to-table movement.

After the war, during the late 1940s to 1970s, many working middle-class Americans increasingly migrated from larger cities to suburban areas. Due to this population and geographical shift, the agricultural industry struggled with trying to meet the increased

Canning fresh foods produced through the victory gardens further promoted self-sufficiency and helped safeguard against food shortages during wartime.

food demands of people around the country. Developments in food processing and transportation technologies made accessing food more convenient. Not only could large wholesale food suppliers readily ship food over longer distances, but they were also able to transport food that lasted longer, was more affordable to the consumer, and could be prepared faster. Furthermore, marketing campaigns encouraged the consumption of more processed foods than fresh foods, which ultimately became the dietary preference of the growing population.

That is, until the nutritional value of these processed foods became a concern. Many Americans became increasingly frustrated with the quality of food (food safety, food economics, and food freshness) that was made available to them. As processed foods with lower nutritional value became the norm in the United States, so did health challenges. Consequently, a growing desire for a food reawakening took place, a hunger for what was considered wholesome, nutritious, and ethical. This growing hope was further promoted by environmentalists, activists, and even restaurateurs like Alice Waters. Because she advocated for the use of fresh and locally farmed foods in her restaurant, she became known as one of the pioneers of the global food movement termed "farm-to-table."

As this concept of choosing farm-fresh over conveniently processed food swept across the nation, households began to consider their own access to more fresh and wholesome foods. Similar to those who created the victory gardens, people around the country became empowered to construct edible gardens right outside their home to address their lack of access to healthier options. This movement has continued on into the present day and is now known as the garden-to-table movement.

Though this lesson highlighted the history of the United States, you may find that the theme of freedom through food resonates with other countries around the world. The fight for food is global, but edible gardens have the ability to help. There's no doubt that we all have to eat, but empowerment will help us create the freedom we need to eat well.

Gardener Ron Finley once said, "Growing food is comparable to printing your own money." I also believe that growing food lays a pathway to freedom.

Next page: Growing diverse vegetables and fruits increases the opportunity for you to consume foods that are best for you and holds deep cultural significance.

Parsley and sage are commonly used in culinary recipes, but these herbs have been used extensively and for a wide variety of purposes in many cultures throughout history.

THE FREEDOM OF HOMEGROWN FOOD

For centuries now, food has healed souls and unified cultures around the world. Think about it: Wherever there are people, food is typically in the midst or brought up in conversations. This emphasizes not only the role that food has in people's ability to connect to one another but also the evolution and prosperity of humans in general. Good food holds immense power, as it can modulate biological functions and create bridges of friendship and harmony, all in one meal.

What is even more interesting is how food has become a means to define cultures around the world. I bet if you were to take the same type of pepper to twenty culturally different places and ask them all to prepare a meal with it, you would get twenty different delicious dishes. And many of these meals would be based upon the history and spirit of the various cultures. For a long time, cultural preferences and needs have defined which types of foods are most valuable and predominantly eaten.

This is ultimately what makes certain food items and meals culturally significant. Now understanding how food can impact the health and evolution of people and cultures, getting access to necessary foods almost seems fundamental, right? Homegrown foods, depending on what you grow, grant you the freedom to connect with the foods that have deep cultural history, even your own history.

Growing foods that you identify with or that are deeply rooted in your upbringing, ancestry, or heritage may not only increase your likelihood of eating the nutritious foods you grow, but it may also further connect you to a part of your identity or what makes you who you are. For this reason, over the years, I have chosen to grow certain food staples in my garden that remind me of my Louisiana family. As a matter of fact, half of my family is from the heart of New Orleans, and cooking Cajun and Creole foods with fresh ingredients runs deep in my blood. Each dish is attached to accumulated stories of the past, and it brings honor to incorporate them into my diet. Many of these Cajun and Creole dishes involve what is known as the "holy trinity," which is onions, celery, and green peppers. Additionally, okra and cayenne peppers are commonly used in many of these dishes, so all of these vegetables are grown in abundance in my garden. The same can apply to you as a gardener as you grow what is familiar and most significant to you.

The late civil rights activist Fannie Lou Hamer said, "If you give a man food, he will eat it. But if you give him land, he will grow his own food." She made this statement as she was launching the Freedom Farm Cooperative. What this implies is that it's one thing to have access but it's another thing to create access. You see, homegrown food can provide you with a direct connection to the foods you rely on and give you the freedom to eat the foods you need with fewer conditions or limitations. Therefore, possessing the capacity to eat the things that align with who you are and what you need is a necessity. Possessing the source is freedom. No matter what space you have, whether it is acres of land or a balcony, whether it is temporary or permanent, the door to food freedom through growing your food is open for you. It's just up to you to walk through it.

One side of my family is from New Orleans, Louisiana, and here they often prepare dishes with okra. One of my favorite recipes happens to be a hearty bowl of Cajun gumbo, which my paternal great-grandmother passed down.

PERSPECTIVES OF A GARDENER

Meet Brian Truong
Location: California
Social Media Handle: @neverenoughdirt
Website: neverenoughdirt.com

Brian in front of his home in California.

MY GARDENING JOURNEY

Gardening has always been a part of me since I was a child. Though the memories of the first four years of my life living in South Vietnam are limited to a few short, fuzzy snapshots of my maternal grandfather's home in the countryside, I can recall a unique gardening memory from over thirty years ago. My family and I spent six months in the Philippines Refugee Processing Center (PRPC) as part of the protocol for immigrating to the United States. My earliest memory of engaging in gardening was there in the community garden plot. Of the different plants growing in the space, I vividly remember the tomatoes and marigolds. So, from then on I cannot think of a time when gardening didn't take place, even when my family arrived in the United States. Once we were in this country, my older brother and I used to watch a popular gardening television show called *The Victory Garden* that encouraged us to try our hand at growing plants.

It wasn't until I got older and acquired space of my own that I became more conscious of sustainable gardening practices. Though small, my backyard growing space is connected to a large undeveloped area and prone to pests like gophers and ground squirrels. While the pests are an annoyance, I was not depending on my garden to fully provide my food at that time, as I was a hobby gardener. That is, until I moved a few years later and increased my gardening space from 60 square feet to 4,000 square feet (5.6 to 372 square meters).

MOTIVATION TO BEGIN

Gardening started out as a hobby and something that I always saw out of my peripheral vision, from the fuzzy image of my grandfather's home in the countryside to the garden plots in the refugee camp and the gardening lessons provided by Roger Swain, host of *The Victory Garden*. The motivation to become my own food producer came many years ago, during a time when the effects of the Great Recession in the United States were still lingering. I decided to become a stay-at-home parent, and when I looked ahead to the future of food production, I saw that growing and cooking my own food was a necessity and a path to

Brian seeks to cultivate his in-ground edible garden using harmonious growing methods and consciousness not to disrupt the balance within his local ecosystem.

freedom. Since that time, I have made it my mission to grow and cook my own food, and each step of the way I am always looking to enhance my gardening skills and increase my efficiency.

Growing my own food has had a profound and positive impact on my wellness and well-being, especially more recently. With the global challenges caused by economic recessions and public health crises, maintaining an edible garden is serving as a buffer against the stress of accessing quality food. The practice of growing food and becoming better at it is a fulfilling and rewarding form of work that has put my mind in a positive state and me in a place where I can provide a positive voice. For my kids and my wife, I can be the best version of myself. We as a family can be a positive version of ourselves and spread that to others.

EDIBLE GARDENING AND FOOD SOVEREIGNTY

Freedom comes in many forms. We are born free, but it is up to the individual to fund their means of survival. Food, shelter, and water are three basic necessities for survival. If a person can grow and produce their own food, they will have covered one big component of survival. Another form of freedom is autonomy of food choice, and this can be achieved through cultivating your own food in a garden. Our access to food is limited to what is available at the market. As a gardener, I enjoy growing fruits and vegetables that are not available at markets due to the obscurity of these foods and lack of commercial viability.

HOW GARDENING INFLUENCES MY PERSPECTIVE ON FOOD AND THE ENVIRONMENT

Freshness, access, and reduced food waste are the top three things that I value most about homegrown foods. Garden-harvested food simply has an improved feel and taste, and as a home cook, there is nothing better than having fresh ingredients. Conventional gardening practices teach us to grow a bed full of one type of vegetable, which can often lead to excess. However, with my unconventional growing methods, I am able to better limit food waste.

EMPOWERED TO GROW NEW FOODS

There are and have been many types of food that gardening has empowered me to grow. One of the things that I like to say about plants is that "plants are the nexus between nature, people, culture, and history." Corn, for example, is a fascinating plant that encapsulates this saying. Wanting to experience an ancient corn, I endeavored to grow one of the oldest varieties—K'uyu, which is grown in the highlands of Peru. When I harvest K'uyu corn the individual parts of my research come together like a completed puzzle. I can understand how its ecology influences what can be grown. Cooking this corn, I can immerse myself with the people that consume it regularly. When comparing this ancient corn with modern corn, I am better able to see and taste how corn has transformed over time to become what it is today. Each step along the way food evolves with nature, people, and culture. So, through gardening, I have been empowered to truly explore food.

A fresh harvest of peppers, onions, and tomatoes straight from the garden.

Brian's homemade fish tacos made with an older variety of Peruvian corn called K'uyu.

I am learning that the journey to becoming a gardener never ends. In this sanctuary I am able to exude the ever-evolving and yet most authentic version of myself.

CHAPTER 7

LESSONS LEARNED

Virtues Learned as a Gardener

By now, you have gotten a glimpse of what you can look forward to on your journey to becoming a gardener. You've viewed various types of gardens, explored how gardens may fight food insecurity, and embraced the dirt that comes along with gardening. Even more, you observed the value of sowing good seeds on this earth, became empowered to be a good steward of your garden and others, and researched the freedom that comes with growing your own food. I imagine that now, after you've walked through all of these spaces with me, you may be reflecting upon the lessons you have learned along the way.

Some of these topics may have contributed to new knowledge, while others may have simply affirmed things you already know. Regardless, there are many lessons that you can take away from this adventure and apply to your own path. Therefore, as our time together grows shorter, I will describe a few virtuous lessons that you may look forward to as you start or continue your journey to becoming a gardener, beginning with patience.

When growing food, you will learn to respect everything you grow, while also being mindful of waste. Carrot tops are normally discarded, yet they provide just as much nutrition and flavor as their roots.

There are many lessons that gardening can teach you—lessons that can translate into every aspect of your life.

PATIENCE

Exercising patience is a tricky virtue, especially in current societies where efforts with immediate rewards and satisfaction are sought after and praised. The faster you can get something, the better off you are; if the result does not come quickly, you've wasted time that could be used more productively, right? It's a given that urgency is necessary in certain circumstances, but quite often urgency dominates patience unnecessarily, leaving you stressed, burnt out, and occasionally disappointed by unmet expectations. I get it, and this conflict with patience versus urgency can take a toll on the heart and mind. Nevertheless, your garden can teach you greater patience over time. The mere act of planning, designing, and building a garden requires a steady perseverance in order to achieve the outcome that you are looking for. And because you are invested in its success, you may find that you tend to not be as bothered by strict timelines and delays. Possessing the capacity to wait without getting restless and annoyed leads to greater patience. The kale and lettuce seedlings that have been steadily growing in the greenhouse for nearly a month are ready for transplanting into the outside garden beds. There they will grow to full maturity.

Another way the garden may provide lessons in patience is through the care for all the plants you grow. As you can imagine, there are thousands of different types of plants and seeds, and some may require specific types of care. No matter what you do, seeds and plants have a set time at which they optimally develop, and it is important to recognize that as a gardener you should not expedite this. Therefore, dedicating time to learning their needs and how to support their growth and development will surely enhance your ability to be more patient. Of course, the ultimate reward may be what you harvest, but the knowledge gained along the way may occasionally feel like an unexpected immediate reward that keeps you going. Your garden will not evolve overnight, as cultivating it is a long-distance race, not a sprint. So, as your garden grows, you may find yourself valuing every minute change that takes place over time.

Caring for plants teaches you patience in that you can't rush a process that you did not create.

While patiently learning how to properly care for your plants, you will naturally segue into researching ways to care for the environment around you. Though I've highlighted this element several times throughout the book, truth be told, this is no easy task. Nature is both simple and complex, filled with layers of dynamic interactions between living and nonliving forms, and humans will never fully understand it in one lifetime. Yet that's where the excitement lies, because there will always be a new curiosity to explore. The never-ending exploration builds not only patience but also enthusiasm for the journey.

You can see how you may gain patience through caring for your garden plants and the environment around you, but there is one final area that the garden may teach you patience in, and that is with yourself. As you nurture the plants in your garden, you may discover that you are subconsciously nurturing parts of yourself as well. Through the gentle manner in which you handle the life forms in your garden, from the plants and trees to the bees and worms, you may notice that you gradually handle yourself with the same care. Just like your garden, your unique journey will require grace and patience from you. There is no such thing as a perfect time, and if there were that would be predictably boring. Allowing yourself whatever time is needed to grow into the gardener that you seek to be is good in and of itself.

Cultivating broccoli can be tedious, as it can take up to 100 days to grow. Yet while waiting to harvest the crop, you will find that every stage of its vegetative development is an exciting event.

Next page left: Plants like this *Echinacea purpurea* (purple coneflower) take their sweet time to bloom. Nurturing flowers will teach you that with patience comes beauty.

Next page right: Small watermelons growing on a vine. Though they take quite some time to grow, their sweet succulent fruits make the waiting worthwhile.

Being mindful of what you use to care for your plants helps you respect other life forms around your plants. Because of this, I opt for using diluted neem oil, which is a plant-based insecticide that is nearly nontoxic to wildlife.

RESPECT

The second virtuous lesson that you may grow in as you embark on your gardening journey is respect. This one is a major lesson that you will carry inside and outside of the garden. Inside of the garden—better yet, around nature—you will gain and give respect to even the smallest of living things. It may also feel as if something just clicks as you observe how all of these large and small organisms manage to live cooperatively, and then you eventually recognize that everything has its purpose and place in maintaining the health and prosperity of the ecosystem.

Though you may not understand every creature's purpose, being respectful of its existence will help you coexist harmoniously. In addition, the nonliving elements of the earth will provide you opportunities to further understand lessons in respect. The earth has been around for quite some time now, long before you and I, and I am sure that it is a joint hope that the earth will stay around long after we are gone. Therefore, it's important to respect the needs of the place we call home. Gardening will undoubtedly teach you respect for the planet as you become more mindful of how your growing methods directly and indirectly affect the soil, the atmosphere, other creatures, and sources of water.

The garden makes provision for you to grow a wide variety of delicious edible and delightful, nonedible plants. It's this rich diversity that makes gardening such an exhilarating experience. You may be inspired to grow rare and culturally specific veg-

Opposite: Gardening teaches me how to further respect myself as I learn to care for and respect every living thing around me.

Pests and diseases, like the one on this tomato, come with the process of learning how to grow food, but don't let it discourage you. You can respect these occasional challenges and allow them to propel you forward.

etables and fruits, and in that an opportunity will be presented to learn the history of different cultures through food. Because food has the power to educate and connect people, learning about various cultures through the foods you grow may help you honor and gain a deeper respect for people's differences, beliefs, and history. As you extend that respect toward others, you may notice that you are able to value people for who they are, and this can lead to improved well-being, feelings of safety, and mutually beneficial relationships for yourself and others.

The journey of maintaining a garden is filled with many ups and some occasional downs. But recognizing that this ebb and flow is natural will help you appreciate and further respect the process of becoming a more informed gardener and even a better version of yourself for life outside of your garden.

Opposite: Tomatoes are powerful staple foods that may be found in several countries around the world. Yet taking time to learn the history and significance of how they are prepared within various cultures will encourage you to honor and respect the differences in all people.

EMPATHY AND COMPASSION

As you become a gardener, you will develop the inclination to extend compassion to all the green life around you.

Empathy and compassion may be two of the greatest virtues that you will learn as you progress as a gardener. These terms are often used interchangeably, so I want to clarify their differences and why they are important. Empathy pertains to the instinctive ability to take on another person's perspective or feelings. Compassion pertains to feeling a person's emotion, then acting in a way that can alleviate or improve what is causing the emotion. In simpler terms, you can say that empathy may precede compassion.

Through tending to a garden, you must keep living things alive. You will need to learn what is required to get them through every stage of development, and that can evoke much emotion and even a degree of affection. Each time a plant suffers, you may notice that your own emotions mirror the plant. Furthermore, you may notice an issue with some of the bees in your space, and that circumstance may elicit sadness or confusion. In both cases, empathy may be learned. However, an opportunity to exhibit compassion presents itself the moment you allow the emotion to inspire you to find solutions to better the plant or solve the issue of the bees. Gardening thus lays the framework for regularly practicing empathy and compassion. The act of caring for another living thing may encourage you to love selflessly and give authentically, to not only the green life around you but to all living things. Moreover, you may also discover that you're able to appreciate the authenticity that others give to you.

In the same manner, being a steward of the garden encourages you to consistently examine the condition of your garden and the ecosystems outside of your garden. This will become a habit developed over time and will certainly carry on outside of the garden, where you may find yourself frequently examining the human condition with greater sensitivity and empathy. But of course you may not stop at empathy because you are an empowered gardener and the compassion you possess will motivate you to find ways to contribute to the betterment of the human condition and well-being of others.

All in all, your garden will teach you some of the most profound lessons in empathy and compassion in such an organic and fundamental way. These lessons will supply you with invaluable experiences that will help you connect with nature and the people around you in a deeper and more intentional way. Even more, the compassionate trait honed as a gardener will boost your capacity to be more aware of and receptive to the experiences and circumstances of others. And like the example of the suffering plant, you may not just feel the pain of another living being, but could also be moved to find a solution to improve the circumstance causing the affliction.

Like all living things, plants are worthy of compassion, and you can show greater compassion by learning their essential needs and helping them thrive.

Learning conscious pest control techniques requires patience and diligence to understand, as each environment has different needs, but the knowledge gained along the way makes the process exciting.

The fruit of your labor will provide food for today, but the seeds of your perseverance will provide food for tomorrow.

PERSPECTIVE

The last lesson that the garden may teach you is perspective—the ability to see things from a different point of view. Your mind is one of the most powerful and complex organs in your body, which speaks to how incredibly important your perspective is. Your perspective is your individualized way of seeing the world (or in this case, your garden) and it is thought to be formed by your unique experiences, values, and current frame of mind. Isn't that something? This is especially significant now because if you are just starting out in your gardening journey you can expect that the viewpoint you have toward gardening and the world today will most likely evolve and shift as you continue forward. And for those of you who are not new to gardening, I am sure you will agree with these sentiments. This means that where you are today, and the evolution that will take place within you on your gardening path, can perhaps shift the way you view the world.

To further elaborate on how gardening can influence your perspective, there are two things that you may observe—humility and hope. The garden has a way of keeping you in a place of humility. Through growing food and other types of plants, you will be reminded that you are just a small variable in a large equation, and though you are entrusted with their care, you are not the creator of these living things. Humility will help you understand that you are neither better than nor worse than any other organism in the ecosystem. Yet, like every other organism, you are valuable, you have a purpose, and you are needed on this earth. After all, that is why you are here at this moment.

In addition to humility, the garden cultivates hope. Where there may be times of despair, the simplistic beauty and peace of the garden may provide comfort and open your eyes to the greater meaning of life. You will realize that as your garden gently

The food harvested from your garden will most certainly be restorative to your body, but the lessons learned will be transformative for your soul.

encourages a perspective shift, you are able to anticipate circumstances and events with a bit more optimism. Likewise, gardening will become a metaphorical activity that offers enlightenment on many principles that are not just applicable in the realm of horticulture, but outside of this domain as well. Audrey Hepburn once said, "To plant a garden is to believe in tomorrow." This is the epitome of how gardening fosters hope—hope that the seeds you sow today will produce bountiful fruits for tomorrow.

As you become a gardener, the lessons of patience, respect, compassion, and perspective will guide you in uncovering boldness in things that you may have previously feared, discovering confidence in areas that may have been uncertain, and finding peace in the midst of chaos. Ultimately, the journey of a gardener is surely a virtuous one, and one that promises great rewards.

Freshly harvested produce like this 'Giant Red' celery will change your perspective on what is considered good food.

PERSPECTIVES OF A GARDENER

Meet Keegan Clifford
Location: Maryland
Social Media Handle: @keegans_garden

MY GARDENING JOURNEY

It's difficult to pinpoint the exact moment I started gardening because it's always been a part of my life. I remember being surrounded by gardening as a child growing up in Trinidad and Tobago. Back then, my great-grandfather had a garden, and I frequently harvested foods like cassava, cacao, and bananas with him. Fast-forward to adulthood, where my wife and I now live on 11 acres in Maryland, and I started my own garden. In 2015 I built a smaller garden on our property. Because I was just starting this garden, I grew only four okra plants, two tomato plants, one eggplant, and some beans. But over time, I increased my growing intensity and now garden in twelve 6- by 3-foot (1.8 by 0.9 m) beds and one 2- by 17-foot (1.8 by 5.2 m) bed year-round.

Joy exudes from Keegan as he stands in his garden holding a large juicy heirloom tomato.

EDIBLE GARDENING AND FOOD SOVEREIGNTY

To me, food sovereignty is the ability to grow my own food or have full access to fresh produce. It also means that I am not beholden to large, commercialized farm industries. Food sovereignty is something that I believe is very achievable for many people. Many don't realize that the resources for achieving that freedom are available, but it's simply a matter of getting educated on where to find them and getting empowered to actually use them. Starting a backyard garden is a great resource that can be used to achieve greater food freedom. A lot of people have a misconception that they need tons of space to grow food, which isn't true. There are many resources on how to successfully grow in smaller spaces, using methods like small containers and vertical gardening.

Keegan's edible garden consists of thirteen wooden raised beds. Here, he is able to grow food year-round for his family and those in his community.

MOTIVATION TO BEGIN

After moving from Trinidad to the United States, I graduated from high school and college and began my career. At the time, my work commute was almost 200 miles round trip. Ultimately, this work pressure played a major role in the stress and fatigue I was feeling. I tried many types of outlets to help me ground from such long workweeks, to no avail. Then I saw a friend's social media post about her garden. I was immediately intrigued by what I saw, and at that moment a little voice inside of me said, "You should try gardening again." I've stuck with it ever since because growing my own food has influenced my overall wellness and well-being by promoting movement. For me, this movement is key to keeping stress and mental and physical fatigue at bay. We all have times when we want to occasionally sit on the couch and do almost nothing, especially after a long day. Yet, with gardening, I look forward to getting outside no matter what the outdoor conditions may be. Whether it's hot, raining, or windy and cold, I am calmed by simply being outdoors and excited to do something in the garden. It amazes me how my garden has an uncanny ability to help me feel relaxed and at peace.

HOW GARDENING INFLUENCES MY PERSPECTIVE ON FOOD AND THE ENVIRONMENT

Gardening has impacted my perspective on elements of the environment. A garden is not only about plants, but it is also about the soil. If you nurture the soil, you can ultimately turn your garden into a healthy and thriving ecosystem, which is a goal that I strive toward in my garden. I try my best to create a welcoming space for pollinators like birds and various insects.

EMPOWERED TO GROW NEW FOODS

Gardening has encouraged me to further educate myself on different types of foods. I am empowered to research, explore, and grow anything I can get my hands on. Because I enjoy growing food year-round, I work to extend my growing season through timing the transitioning of warm-weather crops, like tomatoes and peppers, into crops that thrive in colder weather, like collards and broccoli. Due to my intense growing method, I have more time to grow various types of edible plants. And while I grow a wide variety of vegetables, I've especially enjoyed planting spinach, arugula, turnips, and a lot of the Asian greens like tatsoi (*Brassica rapa* var. *narinosa*) and bok choy (*Brassica rapa* var. *chinensis*).

I also enjoy the unique varieties of fruits and vegetables that are accessible through homegrown produce. I feel that somehow many societies have gotten away from the essence of good food, and we are so used to conveniently seeing food presented a certain way in stores. But the truth is, food comes in many shapes and colors, and gardening proves that. For instance, we see how common white cauliflower is, but there are more varieties and colors, such as 'Purple of Sicily' and 'Green Macerata' cauliflower. There are purple varieties of carrots such as the 'Gniff', which is grown in Switzerland, and cone-shaped cabbages like the 'Early Jersey Wakefield', and both you may never find in a grocery store.

Keegan standing with a rich display of leafy greens and root vegetables—all produced in his home garden in Maryland.

CHAPTER 8

THE GARDEN GROWS YOU

Appreciating Your Gardening Evolution

As we prepare to walk back to the entrance of my garden, accepting that the end of our time together has come, I must say, you did it, my friend. You have come so far in learning how to become a gardener. Additionally, you've gained tips on how to create greater food security for yourself and perhaps those around you. This path is not an easy one, but it will be one of the greatest and most enlightening adventures you may embark upon. Learning to cultivate a garden is so much more than just throwing seeds and plants into the ground; it truly requires a conscious effort and commitment to stewardship from you, the gardener. However, I have no doubt that you will give that and so much more to your garden and to the environment around you. In these last few moments, it's my hope to expound upon ways the garden may grow you as a gardener, and as a human being. I will also use this time to affirm a few principles that you may find helpful as you carry on in your gardening quest. Are you ready?

Gardening is filled with highs, lows, and everything in between. Nevertheless, all of these are the components of an exciting adventure.

Opposite: The journey to becoming a gardener never ends, yet it yields countless opportunities to mentally, physically, and spiritually grow. In your sanctuary you will be able to exude the ever-evolving and most authentic version of yourself.

APPRECIATING YOUR EVOLUTION

As you grow, make time and space to reflect upon where you began and appreciate your evolution. There is an immense amount of development that takes place within your garden and within yourself, and quite often this evolution feels insignificant. Therefore, pulling yourself out to view your progress from a different perspective will help you appreciate just how far you've come. This is definitely needed from time to time, as it keeps you motivated to continue forward with zeal and optimism.

Now, from everything that was discussed previously, you know that the garden will bring bountiful harvests and many high moments. However, like all things in this world, what goes up must come down. This isn't to say that you will experience down moments often, as they may not happen frequently. But when they do occur, it doesn't mean they will break you. In these challenging moments, recognize and accept that it's all part of the garden's and the gardener's growing process. Though it may not feel like it at times, both the good and the bad moments will make your garden and you stronger and more resilient. I encourage you to commend yourself for pushing through in those moments.

Another way to acknowledge your evolution is by celebrating where you are in the present—after all, it took a lot to get to this moment. The road to where you are today required passion, focus, and

While in your garden, step back from time to time to give reverence to the journey that got you where you are today.

perseverance, but most of all it required a willingness to be here. Without those characteristics, it will be difficult to start and maintain a garden. Becoming a gardener doesn't happen with the snap of your fingers, and if it did, you would miss many insightful moments and invaluable opportunities to mature into the best gardener you can be. Gardening is a labor of love, and the effort and degree of empowerment it took to get to the present are worth celebrating.

The last way you can show appreciation for your growth is by reassuring yourself of where you hope to be. This will be dynamic; as you and your garden grow, so will this vision of yourself. However, the moment you lose hope for the future, you lose motivation in the present. To avoid this, practice self-encouragement to reinforce a healthy perspective of the gardener you hope to evolve into, and this will keep you optimistic and focused on your journey. Make it a regular practice to appreciate your evolution and you will discover that you are building strength and confidence as not just any type of gardener, but a joyfully empowered one.

Gardening challenges, like pests infesting your plants, can cause discouragement, but like my mother used to say, "In all things, give thanks." There's an intangible gift of a lesson learned in the challenging moments.

Opposite: Quite often when we look at gardens we think of how we can grow it, not realizing that the garden possesses the ability to grow us in return.

Even the soil, which sets the foundation for the food and plants that grow in your garden, is deserving of thanks.

GIVE THANKS TO YOUR GARDEN

Many years ago I read a quote from Melody Beattie that stated, "Gratitude unlocks the fullness of life. It turns what we have into enough, and more." You have the ability to transform your perspective simply through the power of gratitude. This is why incorporating the practice of giving thanks into your journey will expand your perspective and help you appreciate the largest of gifts to the smallest of gifts, the tangible goodness and the intangible goodness. Even more, a character of gratitude will help you navigate adversity in your garden with a greater ability to cope and remain hopeful that things will improve. Because, guess what? They will! And fortunately, I will share a few factors that may inspire you to implement the practice of gratitude right away.

The garden will provide you many blessings, such as good food, life lessons, and a healthy outlet, all of which are crucial to overall wellness. The road to acquiring these things will consist of some uncertainties, but gratitude will move you to accept that though the process isn't always pleas-

ing and joyful, all of it is holistically good for your development. Also, appreciating the food that your garden gives, regardless of the amount, will inspire you (and perhaps others observing you) to grow more. Your garden may serve as a healthy outlet to rejuvenate your mind and body, while nurturing yourself and those around you. That alone will lead you to express gratitude for all the elements that contribute to making your green space a nourishing sanctuary and prosperous food haven. Even the organisms that contributed in direct and indirect ways, such as the bees, birds, worms, and fungi, deserve thanks. Each of these may be considered such small living beings, but their role in the garden is meaningful and necessary, and that deserves a hearty recognition. Without these organisms, plants may go unfertilized, thus leading to low food yields, and soil may lack structure and nutrients, thus leading to poor plant health. It's easy to see how the minor gifts may be overlooked, but practicing gratitude helps you notice the small things that you may sometimes take for granted.

Lastly, as I have covered some of the smallest of things, I cannot neglect to cover the most obvious, which are the people around you. As you press on you will deeply appreciate those who provide support for you, whether through their efforts, time, or resources. Gardening is rarely a solo adventure because you need something from someone, whether it be tools, soil, an extra set of hands, or even advice. No matter what it may be, your companionship and interactions with others carry immeasurable worth; expressing your appreciation for them can improve your connection and make them feel valued and respected.

Overall, learning to give thanks as you walk along your own gardening path will influence your outlook on gardening and life. Incorporating gratitude into your gardening ritual may ultimately shift your perspective so that you can easily identify the good and positive things along the way, while humbly recognizing that you are also capable of appreciating and being a good steward of those things.

As you maintain your garden, consider giving thanks in the mundane tasks, as these are the things that will help you and your garden flourish.

Give thanks to the fruits of your garden, as they represent the love and care that went into producing them.

There may be moments where people provide you with support along the way, whether through encouraging words or helping to build your garden. Honoring them with gratitude will allow them to see and feel that they are valued.

No gardening journey is perfect; give yourself the freedom to grow at your own pace.

BE GENTLE WITH YOUR PROGRESS

By now, you may see how gentleness in caring for your plants is necessary for your garden to flourish. Still, sometimes it is easy to forget that, like the plants in your garden, you may benefit from a bit of gentleness toward yourself as well. The way you treat yourself may influence your ability to provide care for your garden and those around you. Therefore, consider yourself and your gardening progress with kindness and the utmost care. In this section, I will cover a few reasons why it is crucial for you to treat your development with the respect and gentleness it deserves.

The first step is recognizing that gardening is not a competition. It's actually one of those rare activities where everyone is considered a winner. The path to how you got here and where you are going belongs to you. You are autonomously building this path and taking the steps forward. Comparing your path to that of another gardener is counterproductive and has little value. As you realize that there is no need to compete with anyone, you will be able to honor where you are in the present and where you hope to be in the future, allowing you to walk your path with greater confidence and a more authentic stride.

Secondly, mistakes come with the garden territory. My mother used to tell me, "If you're not making mistakes, then that means you're not trying." I say the same to you, as mishaps will happen along the way but the only way they are able to occur is if there is an effort in the first place. There are many plant-related instructions and horticultural recommendations that you will have to remember as you learn to grow food and other plants in your garden, and mistakes will occur at some point. But remember, even perfectly built robots and computers glitch and have their blunders. You are no different. Striving to be a perfect gardener is impractical, but striving to be a genuine and persistent one is most fulfilling.

This brings us to the last way you can implement gentleness in your progress, and that is through continuing to be the best version of yourself. Being the best version of yourself is a continuous process, not a destination. In doing so, you may exceed the limits of what you thought you were capable of. Just as you look for ways to improve and steadily grow your garden, consciously commit to improving elements of yourself. Before you know it, you'll be blossoming just like the flowers in your garden oasis.

Sunflowers have a way of radiating hope and positivity over the garden, and are typically the first plants you see when entering a garden.

Be sure to water yourself—like the plants in your garden, you will grow too.

There is a garden within you that will need cultivating too.

CULTIVATE THE GARDEN WITHIN YOURSELF

Up to this point, you've learned how to appreciate your evolution, give thanks to your garden, and be gentle with your progress, so what more is there to learn, you ask? Well, this last point is not so much a lesson as it is an affirmation. As we approach the end of our journey together, this is just the beginning of an incredible journey for you. You will hopefully leave this space informed, empowered, and feeling motivated to either start planning your new garden or continue forward with enhancing the garden you have. Regardless, I hope that you are able to take with you a transformed perspective of how to become a gardener and how to cultivate a flourishing garden, including the one within you.

It may be difficult to picture a garden within yourself, but trust me, one indeed exists. This internal garden may be a metaphorical one, but it is nonetheless a significant one. Like any physical garden, the garden within you needs work, such as tilling, weeding, cleaning, and amending. This is why

it is crucial for you to identify and regularly tend to its needs. Also, similar to your physical garden, these needs may be cyclical and may vary in type and magnitude from season to season. Being mindful of these shifts and prioritizing self-care will help you maintain equilibrium and harmony within your internal garden.

To further ensure that equilibrium within yourself, you'll need to consistently and sufficiently feed your body, mind, and soul. After all, there is only one you and you have to take care of it. So setting aside time to ground your mind, nourish your body with good nutritious foods, and strengthen your soul with joy, compassion, and gratitude will ensure that the garden that grows within you is one that is productive, vibrant, and thriving.

Finally, one of the last and most important ways you can enrich the garden within you is by recognizing the incredible value you bring to this world. Your existence is just as important as the birds in the sky, the microorganisms in the ground, and the oxygen in the atmosphere.

Though this may sound overblown, I am here to affirm that it is not. You have a purpose on this planet, whether you know what it is or not, and your gardening journey may help you further understand how to walk in that purpose and use it for the greater good. You have the power to transform your life, whether it be through cultivating a garden as a hobby or seeking to create greater food security for yourself and those around you. Either way, gardening may put you on a restorative path toward finding a better and more genuine version of yourself.

Just as you feed your body with the good foods of your garden, don't forget to feed your mind and spirit with edifying thoughts and knowledge. As the garden thrives, so must the gardener.

Your health and well-being are similar to that of your garden. In order to thrive, you may require consistent support in the form of nutritious foods and holistic care.

Whether you're gardening as a hobby or for survival, the garden will also present opportunities for you to nourish yourself.

Make room for opportunities to not just grow, but to grow more abundantly.

Whenever a guest departs from my garden, I share a basket of fresh produce as a symbol of gratitude and friendship.

A BASKET OF GRATITUDE

Over the course of this book, you have learned many gardening best practices and how to apply them to your own journey. You have also seen how the garden may offer an empowering means for accessing the quality of food your body needs. You have walked through the spaces of other impassioned gardeners and learned exactly what it means to obtain greater freedom through growing your own food. And lastly, you have discovered the many tangible and intangible gifts that gardening gives along the way. So now our adventure comes to a close, but before you go, I want to share a little something that I like to do when anyone departs from my garden. I typically gather a few of my best fruits, vegetables, and herbs and compile them into a small basket for my guests to take home. I consider it a token of gratitude in exchange for the time that was given to me and my space. I don't know you personally, but I am grateful that you intentionally carved out time to walk with me and learn some lessons on how to become a gardener. Seeing that I would share a basket of food from my garden with my guests, I want to extend the same to you by leaving you with a metaphorical basket of goodies—some of the best takeaways from our time together.

Next page: "We might think we are nurturing our garden, but of course it's our garden that is really nurturing us." —Jenny Uglow

Find the garden type that works best for you and your environment.

The road to greater food security for you and those around you may start with an edible garden.

Don't let the dirty moments in gardening stop you from growing; it's all part of the process.

The types of seeds you sow can influence how well things grow.

You have the power to cultivate what you need to not just survive, but also thrive.

Growing your own food is a reclamation of freedom to live a happy and healthy life.

The journey to becoming a gardener doesn't happen overnight, but it's well worth the time and effort.

Your existence is purposeful and carries immeasurable value in this world, and you should never forget that.

An incredible adventure awaits you. I wish you well on your gardening journey, my friend!

A summer harvest of fresh tomatoes and cucumbers.

Wooden pallets can be upcycled and used as vertical or horizontal planters for growing fresh herbs and flowers.

Pickling 'Purple Top' turnip roots in a vinegar-based brine is a quick and easy way to preserve this vegetable for later consumption.

REFERENCES

Chapter 1: A Garden Defined

"Invasive Species." National Wildlife Federation. https://www.nwf.org/Educational-Resources/Wildlife-Guide/Threats-to-Wildlife/Invasive-Species.

Labenz, A. Tyler. "Earthworm Activity Increases Soil Health." Natural Resources Conservation Service, Kansas. https://www.nrcs.usda.gov/wps/portal/nrcs/detail/ks/newsroom/features/?cid=stelprdb1242736.

Raymond, Christopher M., et al. "Exploring the Co-benefits (and Costs) of Home Gardening for Biodiversity Conservation." *Local Environment* 24, no. 3 (2019): 258–73.

Thompson, Richard. "Gardening for Health: A Regular Dose of Gardening." *Clinical Medicine* 18, no. 3 (2018): 201–5.

Wagg, Cameron, et al. "Fungal-Bacterial Diversity and Microbiome Complexity Predict Ecosystem Functioning." *Nature Communications* 10, no. 1 (2019).

Chapter 2: Creating Your Food Security

Ayala, A., and B. M. Meier. "A Human Rights Approach to the Health Implications of Food and Nutrition Insecurity." *Public Health Reviews* 38, no. 1 (2017).

Calancie, L., et al. "Nutrition-Related Policy and Environmental Strategies to Prevent Obesity in Rural Communities: A Systematic Review of the Literature, 2002–2013." *Preventing Chronic Disease* 12 (2015).

"Food Security." Food and Agriculture Organization of the United Nations. Policy Brief. Issue 2. June 2006. https://www.fao.org/fileadmin/templates/faoitaly/documents/pdf/pdf_Food_Security_Cocept_Note.pdf.

Galhena, Dilrukshi Hashini, et al. "Home Gardens: A Promising Approach to Enhance Household Food Security and Well-being." *Agriculture & Food Security* 2, no. 1 (2013).

Seguin, R. A., et al. "Farm Fresh Foods for Healthy Kids (F3HK): An Innovative Community Supported Agriculture Intervention to Prevent Childhood Obesity in Low-Income Families and Strengthen Local Agricultural Economies." *BMC Public Health* 17, no. 1 (2017).

Suarez, J. J., et al. "Food Access, Chronic Kidney Disease, and Hypertension in the U.S." *American Journal of Preventive Medicine* 49, no. 6 (2015): 912–20.

Chapter 3: Getting Down and Dirty

Bradley, Fern Marshall, et al. *Rodale's Ultimate Encyclopedia of Organic Gardening: The Indispensable Green Resource for Every Gardener*. Emmaus, PA: Rodale, 2017.

Conway, Tenley M., and Kyle Brannen. "Who Is Tending Their Garden? Edible Gardens as a Residential Landscaping Choice." *Cities and the Environment* 7, no. 2 (2014).

Reber, Stefan O., et al. "Immunization with a Heat-Killed Preparation of the Environmental Bacterium *Mycobacterium vaccae* Promotes Stress Resilience in Mice." *Proceedings of the National Academy of Sciences* 113, no. 22 (2016).

Rydzewski, Jennifer. "Solutions to Common Garden Challenges." Forest Preserve District of DuPage County, April 16, 2018. https://www.dupageforest.org/blog/garden-challenge-solutions.

Thompson, Helen. "Early Exposure to Germs Has Lasting Benefits." *Nature*, March 22, 2012.

"Vegetable Planting Guide and Recommended Planting Dates." Virginia Cooperative Extension. Publication 426-331. http://pubs.ext.vt.edu/426/426-331/426-331.pdf.

Chapter 4: Sowing Good Seeds

Dowdy, Sharon, and Robert Westerfield. "Fall Gardening: A Collection of Information and Resources." University of Georgia Extension, October 1, 2010. https://extension.uga.edu/publications/detail.html?number=B1432&title=Starting+Plants+From+Seed+for+the+Home+Gardener.

Ferguson, J. M., et al. "Seed and Seed Quality." North Carolina State Extension Publications, January 1, 1991. https://content.ces.ncsu.edu/seed-and-seed-quality.

Kauffmann, Rona. "Maximizing Your Vegetable Garden." Penn State Extension, June 3, 2020. https://extension.psu.edu/maximizing-your-vegetable-garden.

Navazio, John. *Organic Seed Grower: A Farmer's Guide to Vegetable Seed Production*. White River Junction, VT: Chelsea Green Publishing, 2012.

Solomon, Steve. *The Intelligent Gardener: Growing Nutrient-Dense Food*. Gabriola Island, BC: New Society Publishers, 2014.

Chapter 5: Empowerment Through Growing

Artmann, Martina, et al. "Urban Gardening as a Means for Fostering Embodied Urban Human–Food Connection? A Case Study on Urban Vegetable Gardens in Germany." *Sustainability Science* 16, no. 3 (2021): 967–81.

Gregis, Anna, et al. "Community Garden Initiatives Addressing Health and Well-Being Outcomes: A Systematic Review of Infodemiology Aspects, Outcomes, and Target Populations." *International Journal of Environmental Research and Public Health* 18, no. 4 (2021): 1943.

Hale, James, et al. "Connecting Food Environments and Health Through the Relational Nature of Aesthetics: Gaining Insight Through the Community Gardening Experience." *Social Science & Medicine* 72, no. 11 (2011): 1853–63.

McKeon, Nora. *Food Security Governance: Empowering Communities, Regulating Corporations.* New York: Routledge, 2015.

Mura Paroche, Manon, et al. "How Infants and Young Children Learn about Food: A Systematic Review." *Frontiers in Psychology* 8 (2017).

Wilson, Amanda DiVito. "Beyond Alternative: Exploring the Potential for Autonomous Food Spaces." Wiley Online Library, July 27, 2012.

Chapter 6: Freedom Through Food

Benjamin, Darryl, and Lyndon Virkler. *Farm to Table: The Essential Guide to Sustainable Food Systems for Students, Professionals, and Consumers.* White River Junction, VT: Chelsea Green Publishing, 2016.

D'Abundo, Michelle L., and Andrea M. Carden. "'Growing Wellness': The Possibility of Promoting Collective Wellness Through Community Garden Education Programs." *Community Development* 39, no. 4 (2008): 83–94.

Ochel, Evita, and Elaine R. Ferguson. *Healing & Prevention Through Nutrition: A Holistic Approach to Eating and Living for Optimal Health, Weight, and Wellness.* Matrix Fusions, 2018.

Porter, Christine M. "What Gardens Grow: Outcomes from Home and Community Gardens Supported by Community-Based Food Justice Organizations." *Journal of Agriculture, Food Systems, and Community Development* 8, Suppl. 1 (2018): 187–205.

White, Monica M. "Sisters of the Soil: Urban Gardening as Resistance in Detroit." *Race/Ethnicity: Multidisciplinary Global Contexts* 5, no. 1 (2011): 13–28.

Chapter 7: Lessons Learned

Biggs, Matthew. *Lessons from the Great Gardeners: Forty Gardening Icons and What They Teach Us.* Chicago: University of Chicago Press, 2016.

Chapter 8: The Garden Grows You

Emmons, R. A., and A. Mishra. "Why Gratitude Enhances Well-Being." *Designing Positive Psychology* (2011): 248–62.

PHOTO CREDITS

All images from Takia Lamb except:

Keegan Clifford: pages 178, 179, 181

Resh Gala: pages 86, 87

Jasmine Jefferson: pages 54, 55

Misilla dela Llana: pages 114, 115, 117

Shutterstock: pages 18, 26

Deanna Talerico: pages 138, 139, 141

Ashlie Thomas: pages 17, 65, 66, 77, 78, 102, 103, 104, 106, 109, 144, 145

Brian Truong: pages 160, 161, 163

We built and grew this space together, and as a result it has grown us in ways that we could not have anticipated.

ABOUT THE AUTHOR

A few years ago, Ashlie began her gardening journey with her husband on their one-acre North Carolina homestead. Through gardening, she has become more conscientious of local food systems and the health of the environment. Her love for wellness and the environment fueled her passion to grow food and bring awareness to issues of food insecurity in vulnerable communities around the country.

After spending many years in a rural community that lacked sufficient access to nutritious foods, she understood that one way to address this barrier is through learning how to grow food and educating others on what quality foods consist of and where they originate. Ashlie believes that her garden may serve not only as a spiritually enlightening place to ground and regenerate, but also as an opportunity to deeply connect and give reverence to what she feeds herself, her family, and her friends. As a gardener, she hopes to empower others to take control of their health and well-being through growing delicious foods.

It has been an honor to have my grandparents along for this journey, and I am grateful that we are making lasting memories as we learn to grow together.

ACKNOWLEDGMENTS

Preparing the words for this book has been an experience in and of itself, but as you may have seen, perhaps it's been a few years in the making as well. This work highlights not only an aspect of my own life but also the story of so many others who are experiencing or have experienced food insecurity. This global food security dilemma is complex, and when you dive into the data, solutions almost seem insurmountable. But I believe one way to address this big problem is by guiding one another and getting motivated to create better food access for ourselves. It's been an honor to write about how gardens influence the foods we consume as well as our perspectives on life and nature.

Of course, I could not tell this story without the support of a few people, beginning with my brilliant husband and best friend, Tyler. I am deeply thankful for his incredible patience and willingness to learn and go down this path with me. Every step of the way he has used his talents and knowledge to get down into the dirt with me and build this garden from the ground up.

To my family, especially my mother, my maternal grandparents, and my parents-in-law, who, in their own ways, planted seeds of gardening within me and encouraged me every day as I wrote this book. From watching my mother care for a house full of tropical plants to helping my grandparents in their backyard garden in South Carolina, I have been surrounded by compassionate plant nurturers, and I do not take their presence for granted.

Now, I must give honor to a few of my ancestors: my late paternal grandmother and late great-grandparents, all of whom were master gardeners and entrepreneurial farmers who laid the agricultural foundation for many members of the family and community. Because of them, I was able to understand the freedom that gardening often presents. Because of the standard they set, I also believed that gardening and growing my own food was possible. It is the greatest honor to continue the legacy.

I would also like to acknowledge every gardener, farmer, researcher, and food worker who recognizes the issues within local and global food systems and creates impactful solutions right where they are, using whatever they have. These groups have taught me and continue to teach me so much as I grow in this domain, and they are some of the most passionate individuals on the front lines working to disrupt and build more sustainable food solutions for all.

And now you, an empowered gardener. Thank you for making space in your day to walk with me through my garden and the gardens of others. Time is precious, and I am grateful that you chose to be here. I hope that this book has empowered you to either start or continue forward on your own path to becoming a gardener. Wherever you are on that journey, know that you are not alone and that there are millions of gardeners cheering you on every step of the way—including me!

Lastly, I leave you with this quote from the late U.S. representative John Lewis: "Freedom is not a state; it is an act. It is not some enchanted garden perched high on a distant plateau where we can finally sit down and rest. Freedom is the continuous action we all must take and each generation must do its part to create an even more fair, more just society." And that is exactly what I hope that we, the gardeners, can do as we seek greater food sovereignty for ourselves and our communities.

INDEX